Most restaurants fail.

Yours can succeed.

These owners will tell you how...

Introduction

Wes Aiken, Tyler Rullman and I own Schedulefly, a software company that helps restaurants schedule, communicate and get organized online. Restaurants are our customers, and like many people, we have a dream to start our own restaurant one day.

Unfortunately, most restaurants fail in the first few years. That's not good for our business – we need restaurants to thrive – and it's not good for our prospects of fulfilling our dream. With that in mind, we decided to uncover what it takes to be a successful restaurant owner. The idea for this book was born.

Restaurant Owners Uncorked is a collection of interviews with a diverse range of owners, such as the legendary and colorful Phil Roberts, founder of Buca di Beppo and The Oceanaire Seafood Room; Scott Leibfried, a high-energy, renowned figure in the culinary industry who is part of the cast of the hit television show, "Hell's Kitchen"; and Chris Sommers, a former Silicon Valley technology executive who makes Chicago-style deep dish pizza (in St. Louis) so well that he was invited to the White House to cook it for President Obama and the first family.

I learned during this process that there isn't a single recipe for restaurant success. It's just not that simple. If somebody tells you they have the secret, run away. They're just trying to help part you from your money. While most of these owners agreed on the importance of ignoring your ego, of putting your staff before everything else, and of treating partnerships like marriages, their opinions varied greatly on most topics.

For example, Jon Myerow of Tria Café and Biba Wine Bar (Philadelphia, PA) does no traditional advertising, and said, "To me the biggest competition is not for customers. It's for staff. If you compete in the labor market and get the best staff, the customers will follow."

Meanwhile, Jim Parker of Red Hat on the River (Irvington, NY) said, "I'm a big believer in advertising. People say, 'I see you everywhere.' Well, they don't. But that's the perception because we are effective with our advertising."

Jon's strategy works for him and Jim's works for him. The interviews that follow will help you determine which strategies will work best for *you*.

This book isn't useful only for aspiring restaurant owners. It also provides practical advice for anybody who currently owns a restaurant or who simply wants to understand and be entertained by reading the business philosophies of 20 successful entrepreneurs. In fact, all of the people I interviewed, even those with the most experience, were excited to read these interviews and learn from their peers. I admire their collective, humble philosophy that there is always room to grow, room to get better at what they do.

As you read these interviews, you'll feel like you are sitting down with the owners over a cup of coffee or a beer, picking their brains and finding out what makes them tick. You'll learn why restaurants don't have to be risky at all, what chain restaurants' collective Achilles' heel is, why having a good CPA is as important as the food you put on the plate, and much more.

At the end of each interview, I've reiterated what I believe to be the most salient points. Read these chapters in any order. Enjoy.

Focus, university towns
& treating staff righteously

Big Red F Restaurant Group
400+ employees
Denver and Boulder, CO
Restaurant owner since 1988
www.bigredf.com

Dave has built a highly successful restaurant group at Big Red F. His restaurants (Zolo Southwestern Grill, LoLa Coastal Mexican, Jax Fish House - two locations, West End Tavern, Centro Latin Kitchen & Refreshment Palace, Happy and The Bitter Bar) are extremely popular and very successful, and if you're in Denver or Boulder, you'd be missing out if you didn't visit them. Dave is genuine, honest, colorful and smart as heck. He talked about why university towns are great places for restaurants, why it's critical to be cautious about who you choose as investors, how important his staff is to his group's success and much more. He's been at it for over 20 years, and he's learned quite a bit along the way...

How did you get started in the restaurant business?

I started at the age of 15, at a little hot dog stand here in Boulder called Mustard's Last Stand. I liked to cook. I liked to eat. And I liked the whole vibe. I continued that through high school, and then I started working at restaurants in Boulder. I worked at a ski area outside of town, and quickly realized that anywhere that is cool, or that you want to be, there's always going to be a restaurant job.

My step-mom steered me toward the Culinary Institute of America – the best culinary school in America – which I graduated from in 1985. I met a girl named Amy there, and we traveled around a lot and found great kitchen jobs along the way. We lived in New Orleans and worked for Michele Foucqueteau at Flaggon's. In San Francisco I worked at Zuni Café in its early years. We walked all around France tasting real food, and we spent summers in Northern Michigan cooking at a private club, where everything you could imagine could grow in a garden and wild in the woods right out the back door.

I worked in Chicago for a few years, and I was also the chef on Malcolm Forbes' yacht in New York for my internship, which was a crazy experience. I had a lot of great exposure to a lot of styles of cooking and cuisine.

When did you open your first place?

Amy and I got married and came back to Boulder in 1988, and we opened our first restaurant, called The Lick Skillet Café. That was a funky little place 10 miles west of Boulder, up a dirt road. I think part of the charm of that was just the unexpected of driving up a dirt road for 10 miles, and then landing in this little cabin, and then all of a sudden having this food that was just the last thing you expected to find up there. It taught me that a great location didn't always have to be at Main and Main. There just has to be a reason to get there.

That situation of cooking up there in that little place, and learning how easy it is to surprise customers has been something that's carried on throughout all of my restaurants. 20 years later, it's a big part of our mantra to all of the new employees: offer the unexpected.

Whether it's buying somebody something, or you're looking at the uncommon movements of their head and anticipating what their needs are before they have them, or simply anything you can do to catch people off guard, it will be memorable for them. That's not just true for restaurants. It's retail. It's a tire store. Any kind of thing you get as a consumer where it's just a little tiny bit more than what the next guy is going to give you, makes a huge impression.

You and Amy had a partnership at The Lick Skillet Cafe, and that partnership failed. Why?

Yes, I sold my share to my partner after a few years.

In the restaurant business, you get passionate people. It's a hardcore tribe. You work hard. You play hard. You spend a lot of time together. I've been divorced for 11 years, and the restaurant business certainly put a strain on my marriage. I know so many people in the same spot. And I was married to someone who got it. She was a chef, and she got the whole biz. But it's just too damn crazy. God forbid you have just one little added load, and you're done.

But, if you get a partnership with two or three people, or God forbid, more than that, and everybody is strong-minded, and strong-willed — because that's why we're all doing what we do, and we all think we know the answer — it's just hard. It's like painting a picture with somebody. It begins as your picture, and you've got a full idea of how you want it to look. This is where the blue's going to go, and this is where the green's going to go, and here's where the two are going to meet.

Then somebody else comes in with a bigger brush, and heavier paint, and heavier tones than what you thought the thing needed — and you're way off track right then and there.

It sounds like one person ultimately needs to be in charge.

I know of a few successful partnerships, like these guys here in Boulder at Frasca. One's the chef, and the other works the front. And it works. It's a killer restaurant, and they're both really good and wildly talented at what they do.

So you know, sometimes it works. Maybe it has to do with intelligence — successful partnerships have a better chance of success if both people are of a like-minded intelligence.

But there aren't a lot of people telling Danny Meyer, Drew Nieporent and Stephen Starr what to do. Rich Mellman learned a long time ago what he likes and what he doesn't like, so everybody who works for him just follows suit and says, "O.K., this is what Richard likes, and this is what he doesn't like, so let's just always play in the realm of what he likes, and we'll all be successful."

So yes, I think you've got to have one person in charge to give yourself the best chance of success. There's got to be a final voice, or there are just too many different opinions on the same thing. I think when you look at restaurant concepts that are really brilliant, and really clear, it's one guy, or one woman, who says, "Alright, I got this. This is what we're going to do."

Do you have partners at Big Red F?

I've got a couple of partners – chef partners – in some of the restaurants. Guys that started off line cooking, and have been with me for 12, 15 years. So they get a piece of the pie, while getting into the whole thing of owning your own place, which isn't always everything it's cracked up to be.

They're starting to realize that you are the last one that gets paid. Everyone else gets an income before you do. There are a lot of people, especially chefs, that want that name "Owner" on their card. Then it finally comes, they're like, "This sucks. I'm just working my ass off, and not getting what I thought I should. I'm making less now than I was before. And I'm a lot more stressed out."

Ownership isn't always everything it's cracked up to be. When it works, it works great. But when it doesn't, it can bring you down pretty hard.

Let's go back to when you started Big Red F. Did you use your own money?

No, I found five couples to each make investments. I had the luxury of interviewing my investors. I made a list of about 30 names of people that I wanted to hit up for an amount of money, and then I had about 15 conversations after the initial 30, and then I got to pick and choose. I whittled it down to five.

This was in 1993, and we opened a restaurant for $135,000. They each put in $25,000, and Amy and I put in $10,000. We took over an existing restaurant location, and did a dining room remodel, so that when you walked in you definitely knew something had changed. But we dealt with all of the existing stuff in the back of the house. All of the furniture. All of the fixtures. All of the equipment. All of the stoves. We used everything. It was an old Swenson's Ice Cream shop, and we had white marble table tops for three years.

You made do with what you had.

Yes. The kitchen equipment was a half a step above camping gear. It was really, really antiquated, and much too small, but that's all we could afford. So then when we could afford to upgrade and improve, we did. And I wish I still stayed true – and hard – to that mantra, because we used to be able to open a restaurant for a $125,000 or $150,000, and then carry a lot of the opening debt from daily income and cash flow.

You didn't stay true to that mantra?

You get a little fat and a little comfortable. All of a sudden you get a different architect and a different this, and a different that, and we spent $1,000,000 opening a restaurant a couple of years ago. It's in a spot that wasn't a restaurant previously, so we had to spend a lot of money to do it. But I just love the whole idea of sticking tight to taking over existing spaces and keeping your overhead low, because it is a high-risk industry, and having that debt load will kill you.

Did you use equity or debt with your partners?

It was all equity. I went to them with a five-concept business plan, and asked them all to participate in the bigger picture.

Most of them said they decided to participate because it wasn't a single concept, mom-'n-pop, make it or break it deal. They saw a lot more potential in a multi-unit restaurant company than in just investing in Dave and Amy to do what they hoped would work.

The first two restaurants in this new company opened within nine months of each other. That was totally not the plan, especially with two little kids at home. But this second space, which is now Jax Fish House, became available. And it's the greatest thing on the planet. Had I blinked at that moment, I would have missed it. Seventeen years later, that thing is just kicking ass, and will for the next 17 years.

Having investors has worked really well for you. Why?

Having a group of partners who are in it for more than one, whom you can go back to for more capital, has been really beneficial to me as the operator. And for them it's been great, because they are investing in the success of more than just one address.

How do you manage that relationship?

I've kept them involved. This is an annuity for them. I gave them a lot of ownership up front, because until you have profits, all you really have is debt and tax liability. So they got almost all of the restaurant at first, until they got their money back with interest. And then it switched, and I own the majority now.

But they're still in it. You know, they're getting a fantastic annual return on these restaurants every year, and will for a long time. Hell, their grandkids will be working at these joints, so it's a great thing for them. And with being able to do things like open a second restaurant nine months after the first, it has been a great thing for me as well.

You interviewed a large group of potential investors, and narrowed it down to five. How important is it to find the right people, and not just the money?

It's critical for anybody thinking about opening up a restaurant to really evaluate who you are bringing on board. You know, the big talker sitting at the end of the bar saying, "Yeah, I got all this money any time you want to open a restaurant," is the last person you ever want to have involved in your restaurant, because that person will be your and your staff's worst nightmare.

I found people that I really respected. People that I liked. And 17 years later, I'm going to ball games with them, skiing with them, traveling with them. I'm having them over for dinner and I'm friends with their kids. In some cases I'm closer in age to their kids than I am to them. They were older, more established business people. None of them were retired and none of them had made fat cash from an inheritance or not doing anything. All of these people made their own money, and are very active, understanding business people. They get it.

None of them were in the restaurant business per se, but they are all in tune and understand how hard the business is, and what's being done, and they're very respectful. They don't come in on the weekends. They steer clear when we're busy. I give them a little tickler of free food every month as part of the investment. So that's great. And the staff treats them really well, and they reciprocate, because they get that the staff is the key to our success.

It's really a great and unbelievable success story as far as partnerships go, because you can get hooked into people that make your life miserable, who have their own agenda. My partners are all dream people to do business with. They're fantastic!

If you are looking for investors, what do you look for and what do you avoid?

Well, it's like going out on a first date. If you're in your mid-twenties, or thirties, and you're dating with something bigger in mind, that's the same as finding an investor. So when you get those weird hits, and those weird personality charges, and those weird ego comments, run fast and run far, because that stuff will only get worse.

There's an interesting dynamic in any industry when it comes to raising money. There's this whole song and dance thing that happens between investee and investor, where when you're hungry for money, you'd wash the guy's car, mow his lawn or do whatever you can do get his or her cash.

And then as soon as they write that check to you, the dynamic changes, to where they're genuinely concerned about your health. They're interested if you're finding enough time to take off. They're worried about your marriage and your health. They want you to spend time with your kids.

It's a funny switch that happens with intelligent, integrity-ridden investors who are in it for the bigger picture. You're always going to have these people that are just totally cash-driven, and they really couldn't give a shit what your personal life is like. But I've been fortunate enough not to have any of those kinds of people involved in my businesses.

So you've really got to think about your long-term success when you're interviewing these investors, because much different than a tech firm or something that you might be investing in, this is a very interactive investment for these people. They're in your place, representing your brand, walking around the community, telling people that they are your partner and an owner.

Man, if they're not walking the high line that you expect them to, then you could be in a really bad situation. Let's say three years into it one of them gets a nasty coke habit and is out nightly hitting on all of your hostesses, you're just like, "Whoa dude, this is all wrong." And they're an investor. They're an owner! You're so screwed at that point.

This is great advice. Most people probably just think about getting the money.

Absolutely. You really have to be crystal clear that this is a business that you're creating. I'm looking at going into my third decade with these people, and I hope to go into the fourth and the fifth. I've stayed with my same group the whole way through. My ex-wife still is a partner, and has invested in all of the stores that we've opened since we got divorced.

For a lot of people, all they've ever wanted to do is own a restaurant. So they are a 10% owner, and they are walking around there like they own the joint, and the staff is drawing straws to see who has to wait on them. It can be a nightmare. I have so many friends with restaurant investors, and it can be just a complete nightmare.

You have to think long term. It's like marrying into a family. You're going to spend time with these people. They're going to see you at your worst. They're going to see you at your best. You're going to have to deliver tough news sometimes. They have to trust you explicitly. And vice versa.

You know, you get some really uptight, really anal business guy whose questioning every dime you're spending, and wanting to scrub the books all of the time, and it's an absolute nightmare.

Have any of the Big Red F restaurants failed?

We've had one go under, which was called The Blue Plate Kitchen. It was great, but in a bad location. Kind of cursed. People still talk about that food, but I was going through a divorce at that time, and in this business, when you take your eye off the ball – even for a moment – things change. It doesn't always mean they are going to change for the worse, but they are definitely going to change, whether you like it or not.

That was just a time where I was not on it. I had the wrong managers, the wrong kitchen people, and it just never worked. We started listening to everyone who had a comment on what they thought was the problem, what they thought we should change, and the place became wildly schizophrenic. We didn't even know what the hell the place was anymore. Every time a customer walked in, it was different.

It was open for about a year and a half, but it was clear that it needed to close. So we shut it. But that, knock on wood, was the only square egg we've laid.

Why are university towns good places to open restaurants?

Man, the college environment in this town, and in a lot of towns where universities are thriving – like Ann Arbor, Madison and Austin – is a fantastic scenario for restaurant success. You've got 5,000 to 10,000 new kids coming in every year, and their 20,000 parents.

In the case of CU (University of Colorado), it's really a major driving force of the economic vitality of Boulder, in a great way. And every year you get all of these new kids, and they've got mom and dad's gold card, and they're trying the restaurants to see what's what, and their parents are coming in to visit them, and then they finally turn 21 as a junior, and then they're really ready to see what it's all about. It's nuts. It's awesome.

How do you find people to work for you that will have the same passion for your restaurants that you do?

Well, it's just like in any successful thing, be it a band, or a football team. We've always had the attitude that you'll never have happy customers unless you have happy employees. So all of our focus, first and foremost, is with the employees. You treat them well, you treat them with respect.

Take things like Schedulefly. That's a respect move on our part, to spend a little bit more money to make the staff's lives easier. So these people can now have access via the Internet to their schedule. They don't have to call and interrupt. They can make plans. They can have a life. It gives them some control around the outcome of their lives outside of work.

For us, it's always been about creating an environment where people want to work. And then you just maintain it, and the doors are busting down from people who want to be on the team, because the team's got a great reputation. You have to hire intelligent people, and then expect them to be world famous.

I can tell that's a really big deal to you.

Absolutely. Look around at any successful restaurant or at any successful store. Walk in to a Nordstrom's, or The Ritz Carlton, and you see that staff walking around. They're intelligent, smiling and engaging. They're looking at you in the eye. As a customer, you're thinking, "I want to live here. I want to sleep over there in the corner, and just hang out with these people, because they're fun."

So it's a very common sight after dinner to see customers hugging our wait staff, hugging our bussers. We've even had a lot of inner-company weddings.

We're asking people into our home. And just like if you had a great friend over you haven't seen in a while, you make sure your stuff is together. You make sure the music's dialed, the temperature is comfortable, the lighting is appealing. You make sure everything in your refrigerator looks like the greatest thing they could ever put in their mouths. Make sure you're taking care of your friends just like you would if your girlfriend's mom came over for the first night for dinner at your house.

You mentioned how important it is to treat your staff really well...

We've never run into issues with people quitting and storming out. By the time someone's about to be fired, you know, it's a mutual thing. We're shaking hands, "Yeah, it doesn't work for you. It doesn't work for us. We're good. You can roll on and we'll actually help you get your next job."

If we're assholes to our employees, we wouldn't have anybody. You can't be a jerk. I know so many restaurant people that have their ego as the driving force behind what they are doing, and then they pay for it when people do things like steal from them.

We don't have any of those issues, because it's just a big family. We don't have security cameras in the restaurants. We don't check cash drawers and pull drawers in the middle of shifts like a lot of places do, or check backpacks as employees head out the door at night. I just can't believe that. Employee theft is just not even on our radar. How could somebody want to clip you when you've just done them so righteously all of the time?

What are some of the things you do for your staff?

We have killer employee parties. We give all of the staff 40% off when they come into the restaurants. We're always doing some sort of killer promo, or we're making all kinds of crazy T-shirts, or throwing them all kinds of perks.

I'm one of the dinosaurs who still pays 100% of the managers' health insurance, so that's been a big key of people sticking around too. It is something we will always do, and it makes a big statement to the people who work their asses off in these stores.

You also have a unique policy of paying staff to do volunteer work.

Yes, I pay my staff $10 per hour to do community volunteer work, for up to 10 hours. It doesn't sound like a lot, but it's $45,000 per year if they all took me up on it.

But if we pay $1,000 per year to people for doing that, it's a big year. The majority of the volunteer work done is by the older staff. So it's a shame, but at least we're putting it out there, and telling people, "Whether you're here for a year, or you're going to stick around after college, this is your community. When people need help, this is what you do." That has an effect on people. If they go out and do it or not, they know they are a part of a cool team who is trying.

I keep hearing that ego can be a problem with owners.

You can see it from across the room. You can see it in the way the staff interacts with this person. It's so evident and obvious when that kind of vibe is going on, because the staff is just uneasy. They're not at ease. They're not feeling it.

It's important to take care of your crew, and to mean it, because they're not dumb. You can't fake them out, like you really give a shit. You gotta walk that walk.

Why is the failure rate so high in your industry Dave?

Well, it's getting tougher to impress. It's getting tougher to find great locations. But these stats and these figures of a 4% success rate, or that 90% fail in the first year, are because a lot of people cook, and they're think, "Wow, I'm a great chef. I'm going to open a restaurant."

But good food is just the start of it. There's managing people, schedules, shift notes, tax deposits. There are quarterly income sales taxes. There are so many balls in the air when you are running a restaurant, and it's so easy to drop three or four. When you drop them continually, you're not a juggler anymore. You're just a guy with a ball in his hand.

You get these people for whom money isn't an issue. Dad's got a fat bank account, and he or she is going to open this great restaurant. But they don't have the work ethic, and they don't have the business sense to be thinking the way they should be.

What should they be thinking?

They should be thinking, "Wow, I'm going into an industry where banging an 80-hour week is not going to impress anybody, because that's what I have to do every week. And I've gotta really pay attention and hire the right people. I can't act like I know everything, because I don't know how to add two plus two, so I need to hire an accountant or a bookkeeper or a CFO who's really going to steer me in the right direction.

I don't know anything about wine, even though I'd like everybody to think I do, so I'm not going to try and write the wine list, I'm going to hire somebody who is smarter and better and faster than I am. I'm going to write a badass wine list with this person, letting him take the lead and own it. When we get some press and the reviewers walk in, my wine expert is the one whose picture is on the cover of Wine Spectator, and that person will be with me forever because he is going to feel a sense of ownership."

You just have to get the ego out of the way and be smart about business. But that doesn't happen a lot. Everybody thinks they know everything, and before they know it, they're done.

That show "Hell's Kitchen" with Gordon Ramsey is classic. Every time he walks in there, and these guys are saying, "Oh yeah, that's not right. That's not going to happen." And after a half an hour of every show he's like, "Look. I'm here to help you. You can either listen to what I'm telling you, because I know what the hell I'm talking about, or I'm just going to walk out. I'm gone. You're good. Congratulations. Best of luck to you."

That's tough!

That's the way it is. This industry, more so than others, is full of passionate people. Sometimes it's passionate people who really get it, and understand it, and they're making good decisions. And then there are complete passionate idiots who don't know what the hell they're doing.

"Passionate idiots," huh? That's a recipe for problems.

You can lose money fast in this business. I mean it's amazing how behind the ball you can get in a short amount of time. It adds up quick. The numbers are real, you know? You've got an average restaurant with 100 seats doing lunch and dinner seven nights a week, a wait staff of 10 or 12 people with six bussers, 10 cooks, four bartenders, three or four dishwashers, a bar manager and two store managers. That's a $15,000-per-payroll commitment. More with payroll taxes.

So every other week, you're on the hook for $15,000 or $16,000. Fall behind one week, and you're behind the eight ball. Then a snowstorm comes, and you get minimal business. And you bought too much food, and you've got way too big of an inventory, so then you didn't make payroll last week, and then you got killed on the weather this week, and boom. You know, you're really under the gun. Then you're spending the next 60 days solving the problems that you created over the last 10. And let's just hope nothing else goes wrong in the next 60 days.

Before you know it, you're saying, "Wow, we lost $20,000 this month, and we've got this bill coming up. We've got this bank loan that we're going to be behind on." All of a sudden, this, that, and the other happen, and you're $70,000 in the hole, seven months into a restaurant.

You're thinking, "Oh my gosh." And then you have that $1,000,000 decision of, "Do we just bail right now and only lose $70,000? Or do we convince ourselves that we can correct this ship, and get it right again?" So you try to correct it, and in a year and a half, you're $200,000 in the hole. Then you're really screwed, because you can't go home to Christmas dinner because you've got all of this hard-saved money from your parents uncles and aunts invested in this thing that's going south in a hurry.

How do you come up with ideas for new concepts?

It all usually gravitates around seafood and Mexican food in my world. "Doing something common, uncommonly well" is what our director of operations John Bachman always preaches.

We're just trying to offer people something that isn't available. You don't want to be the tenth place doing something. You want to be the first. If it is something that is already being done, then you better be the best.

The West End Tavern has one of the biggest bourbon selections in the country. We're doing a little bit different take on southern barbecue, burgers, mac-n'-cheese, and collard greens. A bunch of old school, simple comfort food. Nothing revolutionary. But we're just doing it well, and doing it every day.

But it's always first and foremost food. If you don't have great food, you will not succeed. Period.

What's on your mind for the future?

Just trying to fine tune, and not getting too cocky with how things are kicking ass, and not getting ahead of ourselves.

I was really close to pulling the trigger on a space in Ann Arbor, MI and I'm still looking at that, for a Jax. But I'm taking just a little bit longer look, to make sure that we're not getting ahead of ourselves. The conservative, hyperactive part of me feels like the worst is yet to come on this whole recession, and that there could be another blip on the screen that's not nearly as long, but terribly devastating to people who have been hanging on for the last 24 months.

I don't want to be in the middle of a construction project six states away if that's going to happen. So we're chilling right now, and just trying to make these joints better, which is a full time job.

Highlights – A quick recap of Dave's key points...

- ✓ Things change when you take your eye off the ball, even for a moment

- ✓ Ownership ain't easy street

- ✓ Go where the universities are

- ✓ Your investors will represent you in your community – choose wisely

- ✓ Treat staff righteously

- ✓ Don't be the tenth restaurant doing something – be the first

Raising money, community
& the Achilles' heel of restaurant chains

Top of the Hill Restaurant & Brewery
100+ employees
Chapel Hill, NC
Restaurant owner since 1996
www.thetopofthehill.com

Scott Maitland started Top of the Hill Restaurant and Brewery to prevent a chain restaurant from dominating downtown Chapel Hill. Not only did he accomplish that, but he turned his restaurant into a place that represents the quintessential Chapel Hill experience. Located at the very heart of downtown Chapel Hill, Top of the Hill Restaurant & Brewery is, quite simply, the social crossroads of Chapel Hill. It has undoubtedly become an institution. Here's how Scott made that happen...

Why do you own a restaurant?

I was an Army officer and I had the worst company commander in the history of the Army. He almost got me killed twice for no other reason than he was incompetent. I decided at that point that I would never let somebody stupider than me be in charge of me again. I'm not saying that I'm smart. But I figured if you are stupider than me I don't want you in charge of me! [Laughs]

So I decided to be a small business person, and I knew I wanted to live somewhere in the South. In my second year in law school at Chapel Hill, I realized that was where I wanted to stay. I found out that the landlord of the building we are in had announced that he was going to put a TGI Fridays in the middle of downtown Chapel Hill. And even though I had decided just a week earlier to live in Chapel Hill, I couldn't let a chain restaurant dominate downtown Chapel Hill.

How did you come up with a concept?

I had recently become inspired by a U.S. News & World Report article about the rise of Starbucks in '94 when Starbucks was a new thing. The article also pointed out these new phenomena of microbreweries and microbrew pubs were doing pretty well wherever Starbucks and other "upscale" coffee houses were located. I was sitting in a coffee shop reading this article, and the owner walked out and said he was going out of business, but that two "upscale" coffee houses were opening up down the street soon.

He used that same term, "upscale", as the article used. Wherever "upscale" coffee houses did well, then microbreweries seemed to do well. So the light bulb went off in my head, and I decided I could start a brew pub at that corner and prevent a chain restaurant from dominating downtown Chapel Hill.

You were still in law school then?

Yeah I was in my second year in law school. I had absolutely no experience with restaurants and no money! [Laughs] I was class president, and I was on a full academic scholarship, and I was trying to start this on the side.

So what happened next?

A lot of flailing around actually. I was very serious. I wasn't casual about doing it. But I literally had no experience and no understanding of what it would take. So I realized that nobody was going to take me seriously, because I had no experience and no money. I knew I would need to raise money, and in order to do that I would need to create a team that people could buy into. To do that, I started looking for somebody that knew the beer world, and somebody that knew the restaurant world.

Not to delve too much into this one day, but it was a critical eight hours. I literally sat in the coffee shop and found out about the landlord putting in the chain restaurant, and I decided to do something about it. I went home, and luckily I had access to LexisNexis as a law student. Remember this was 1994, before Google and all of the easy search. LexisNexis enabled me to pull up every article that had been written in the last five years about brew pubs and micro-brewers, and it gave me 872 articles.

That's quite a bit of content to sift through!

It was. But I sat down at midnight with a legal pad and read every one of the articles and took notes. By 6 o'clock the next morning I swear I was the most knowledgeable man in the brewpub industry.

I was able to pretty much see the whole history of the industry in that five year period, and I got to see the rise and fall of individual brew pubs, and I learned lots of lessons. One of the things that I recognized was that, in my mind, brewpubs that were successful were what I called fourth-generation brewpubs.

During the first generation it became legal, and guys just attached them to a pizza place or something. Second generation, they build a larger space for the brewery but they weren't really committed. It was more of a part-time thing. Third generation, people focused on the breweries and kind of short changed the restaurants.

I realized that the key to success was going to be creating a fourth-generation brew pub that had a top of the line restaurant and a top of the line brewery.

So as I'm reading though these articles, those ideas are coming through my brain. And then the last article I read is about the publisher of "All About Beer" magazine, Dan Bradford, having moved the headquarters of the magazine from Boulder, CO to Durham, N.C. the year before. I realized that, *My God, this is going to work.*

What did you do next?

I called Dan and asked him to have lunch with me. He told me that he had been approached a number of times by people that wanted to do something, but nobody really had the knowledge base. Luckily, I had that knowledge base because I had just read all of those articles the night before, and I had all of this knowledge and some good ideas as far as he was concerned.

We originally started out with him as a consultant. But I didn't have any money, so I ended up making him my partner. And it's been a great partnership. Dan is a great beer critic and a magazine publisher. He'll be the first to tell you he's not an expert brew master. But he gave me tons of credibility in the beer world. He knew how to find a brew master, and he knew how to find equipment manufacturers. He also knew hundreds of brew masters, so if we had a problem, he knew who to call to find out how to solve it. Over the years, Daniel has been key to me in terms of getting information.

So that relationship started pretty early. Then I ultimately ended up becoming partners with my best friend from high school, and that didn't work out so well. I would caution people to really think about the skill set that people bring to the table when you make them a partner. But through him I was also able to find a restaurant in New York City that also agreed to be our partner. So then we had the team.

At the same time I was learning some hard lessons about how to financially structure the deal. I studied LLCs [Limited Liability Corporations] in law school, and realized they allowed us a lot of flexibility to set up a company and take advantage of tax laws and limited liability.

So a lot of things were coming together. After talking to literally hundreds of people about investments, and refining my concept in terms of how to financially structure the project, after two years I was able to finally raise the full $1,200,000 and it took six months to build it.

How much of your team's money was in it, and how much did you borrow?

My father had passed away that year. I inherited $50,000 dollars from him and I used that. There wasn't much other money put in. We borrowed the rest. Ultimately, Joseph Smith, my restaurateur partner from New York, had to put in hard cash to make the lenders feel better.

Going back to the financial structuring of the deal ... I originally thought I would find 10 people to each give me $100,000. But I realized quickly that $100,000 is the worst amount of money to try to raise. It's more than what the average person has to invest, but it's really small to the person who has a lot of money. As a very rich guy told me, you've got to work as hard for the $100,000 deal as you would for the $1,000,000 deal or the $10,000,000 deal.

So I knew I wasn't going to do this with all equity. I needed some debt as well. I learned about SBA loans and I decided to go for $500,000.

I went to the first bank, and they rejected me. And the next bank rejected me. And the next bank. I learned that I didn't know enough about my product, and how to pitch my deal. I tell my students now – and this is the most important thing I tell them – that if you are going to raise money, you are going to make a list of people that you are going to talk to to raise money, and don't start your pitches with the people at the top of your list. The mistake most of us make is, we start off with our very best prospects. That's what I did, and with no experience with my pitch, I gave lousy presentations, and burned my prospects.

If you are going to make a list, turn it upside down and start at the bottom. By the time you get to your best prospects, you are going to have a much better presentation, and a much better deal. It's not just about showmanship. When you make a presentation and you get rejected, you ask "Why?" You can't get upset, and you have to focus on making your deal better.

How many banks rejected you, and how did you finally get one to lend you money?

I got rejected by 18 banks, and I am now at the 19th bank. And this is an important meeting, because there are no other banks in the freaking area!

So I'm at the 19th bank, and I am asking for my half a million dollars, and the guy says, "I tell you what, if you can raise the other $1,150,000, I will give you $50,000." So that wasn't going to do much for me, but I said, "Great! Put that down on paper for me."

Two days later I went back to bank number 18, and I said, "Hey I just talked to bank number 19, and they are going to give me $50,000, but I like you better and I would like to do business with you." I'll be damned if he didn't give me $75,000. So I said, "Put it in a letter for me."

I worked my way back up the banks, and by the time I got to bank number five, I got a full $500,000 loan. As soon as I got an SBA loan approval, even though it was contingent on me raising the money, it really helped me raise more money. Suddenly now, it was almost like the Good Housekeeping Seal of Approval, because investors could see, "Oh wow, this guy has been approved by a bank – by the SBA. He must be for real."

The other thing I learned is that people are very reluctant to give you cash, because they think you are just going to burn it. You know, spend it without raising all of the money, yada, yada, yada. Again the law school degree was helpful. I created a trust and made my banker the trustee. She was not to release the money unless I had received the full SBA loan. And so that method worked out well, because suddenly people knew that I was not going to run off with their money.

And then, finally, you are going to find when you raise money, people will say "I will be your last $50,000" or "I will be your last "$100,000" or whatever. That happens, again, because I think people are afraid of having their money sit on the sidelines, or of having it be spent. It's kind of a variation of the trust issue. So all I said to each person who said they would give was, "Great, write that in a letter." And when I made my next presentation, I would count that as money that people had given me.

On the day that I had raised all of the other money, I called three different people that had promised me that last investment, and said "Hey, you are the last investment." So there were three simultaneous last investments, and I was able to raise all of the money.

How did you divide the equity?

I created an interesting structure where the sweat equity guys kept 66% interest in the restaurant and the cash guys kept 33%. My rationale was 1/3 for the idea and the work, 1/3 for the personal guarantees on the notes, and 1/3 for the cash. And the way the cash payment was set up was that there was a little bit of a preferred return. I stole some ideas from preferred stock, and so there is a little bit of a bond aspect to it. Not to get into too many details, but the bottom line is that it was attractive to investors, and I was able to raise that money.

Didn't you raise additional money?

Yes. If you ask anybody that knows anything about me raising money for Top of the Hill, they'll tell you about the "Founders Club." The Founders Club was not about raising money though.

It all goes back to being in this particular space. I needed to convince the landlord to give me the space. But the landlord didn't believe that I was going to be successful, despite the fact that I took him and showed him my partner's New York restaurants, and I took him to show him brewpubs in Atlanta.

He just didn't think it was going to work, and he asked me for proof that it was going to work. I was sure that I was going to be unable to provide proof. But in order to show the landlord that we would be successful, I would offer people the opportunity to join a Founder's Club by giving me between $100 and $1,000. That got you a free t-shirt, your name on the wall, and when the restaurant opened, a tab worth twice your investment. I thought 20 or 30 people would join.

Instead, people started joining like crazy. I cut it off at 550 people, after I had raised $75,000. So although it didn't start out being a fundraising effort, I did raise $75,000. That $75,000 wound up being pretty crucial when we first opened.

How critical was developing a solid, well-researched business plan to your success?

I think the business plan was extremely important. But not necessarily for why most people think it is.

Essentially that one night of study allowed me access to the best practices of a new industry, so that was key in terms of the industry. But at the end of the day, an independent restaurant is all about your local community. If you don't understand that local community, then I think you've got real problems.

I have seen very qualified operators trying to come into the Chapel Hill market from out of town. It's very clear that they just don't understand the Chapel Hill market, and that's so important. That intimate knowledge of your local market is key.

I think that business plans and research need to incorporate that as much as anything else. I even made some tremendous mistakes. For example, who was going to write the menu? I'd never written a menu before. So I have my chef from D.C. and my partner from New York work on it. They come up with a menu, and to me the menu looks weird and overpriced. But they assured me that it was great.

Well, it was great for New York and D.C., but not this market. And in fact, it was considered weird. And it was considered overpriced. So we had to change it.

How did you figure that out?

You've got to listen to your customers. There's no way around it.

At the same time – this sounds crazy – you can't let your customers take you away from your vision. For example, I truly wanted to create the social crossroads of Chapel Hill, which was different from what somebody with experience would have done.

There were different groups in Chapel Hill: the faculty; the undergrads; the grad students; the locals. But there was no place for them to intermingle, and I wanted to have a place where everybody could come together. That is counter to the advice that you would get in the restaurant business, which is typically to figure out what your demographic is, and really focus on that specific demographic.

If you're doing what we did, you better know your market. You better know when you're writing your menu that you are writing it for the undergraduate on a date, the grad student on a budget, and the businessman who is coming in to soak up the culture. It needs to be a menu that answers all of those needs.

I now have a much better appreciation of the role of the menu in a restaurant. I think everyone starting a restaurant will tell you that the menu is important, but I don't think people really understand how important the menu is. It drives everything, from staffing and equipment needs, to the type of customers you are going to get, to the whole feel of the restaurant. So you've got to think long and hard to what it is that you want to offer.

Luckily for me, I am in a town where every year we get another bite of the apple. So the first year, I start in September, and I figure out by February that we have to make major menu changes, which we do, but it isn't until the fall of the next year that I get a whole new wave of people in town that are willing to try me out. We were able to get it going after that.

How about an example of a restaurant that didn't have that intimate local knowledge?

Here's one. Michael Jordan hooked up with an independent restaurant group out of Chicago to start "23 Restaurant" here in Chapel Hill. They had marketed themselves as the place for fathers and sons to go to before the game. To be frank, I was a little nervous. They were right down the block, and I was thinking it was going to be tough to compete against that.

Well, I've never seen a group that had such a scattered concept of what the restaurant was going to be about. They were advertising it as the place to go to before the game, but the menu didn't have a hamburger on it. Rather, they were selling $26 rabbit!

I now have this theory that the bigger a city is, the farther it is away from its food, so consequently, the food needs to become more and more exotic. I don't know if I am accurate or not, but I guess rabbit seems fun and exotic in Chicago. Meanwhile, there are plenty of people here in North Carolina who remember hard times, and the only way they got to eat was to go out and shoot a rabbit. So the idea of paying $26 to have a rabbit doesn't work on many levels. It's not what you want to eat before a basketball game, and it's not what this market wants. So that business plan is important from understanding how the business works, but you have to think the whole concept through from soup to nuts.

It also sounds like being consistent with your vision is very important.

You know, the idea of sticking to your guns in terms of your vision is tricky. That can easily be morphed into not listening to your customers. There is no way to know what's right or what's wrong in that area.

I would tell anybody who is trying to do this that they need to really think about the true core of their concept, and hold those core elements sacrosanct. And other than *that*, they need to listen to the customer.

So we want to make our customers happy, but also be individual and unique in doing it. I think in this day in age of better funded and better operated chain restaurants, quite frankly, uniqueness, and just being flat out weird, is the only thing we independents have got left. [Laughs]

What about your staff? How do you find people that will share your passion and your vision and will serve the customers the same way that you would?

That's the key to the operation. We're really lucky that we're 10 yards off of campus, and we get inundated with applications from high-quality young people all of the time. But the biggest challenge we have is to find motivated, qualified folks to take that junior management position. That's tough.

The one suggestion I have is to never hire somebody just to fill a spot. Don't do it. Only hire somebody that you think is going to be good. I think it's better to have no manager at all than to have a bad manager. I really believe that, and I unfortunately learned the hard way.

It's a challenge for an independent restaurant in a college town to provide the potential for upward mobility within the organization, so that people can consider it a career and not just a one- or two- year gig. In no small way, that helped drive our recent expansion, and some other things. We realized on some level that we needed to give a team that has been with us a long time the opportunity to continue to grow in terms of the compensation they receive, and all of that stuff.

You seem to always be on the leading edge of new trends, and you do unique things. Talk about that.

Well first, I don't consider myself a restaurateur. I consider myself a business person. And not to take away any of my passion for our product and the beer and the food and serving customers, but the reality is I think I would have that same passion if I were making a cardboard box or whatever.

I think having had experiences outside of the restaurant business — going to West Point and being in the Army; being Ross Perot's campaign manager in the '92 election in Florida — allows us not to feel trapped by the conventions of the restaurant business itself. That's the reason Top of the Hill is able to do some of the things that other people don't. We look at best practices, and those best practices can come from any organization.

I was on the bleeding edge of guest affinity programs. I tried to launch one with our Founders Club back in 1996. What I learned about that is that I took two bites of that apple, and I don't put a lot of stock into that stuff. I don't think that those types of programs help the restaurant.

We also offered free Wi-Fi before people understood the concept. I had to explain the concept to my staff.

We're also very proud to be, as far as we know, the only bar/restaurant in the South to have its own in-house cask-conditioned ale program that's on constantly. And so that's kind of on the cutting edge of micro-brewing itself. If you don't know what cask-conditioned ale is, it's great. If I had to make a bad analogy, it's sort of equivalent to a single-barrel bourbon. So that's a lot of fun.

We are always looking for new things. To be honest, I was aware of Schedulefly a good year or year and a half before I could convince my managers to use it. I was convinced that it would be helpful in so many ways.

But if you are going to have an organization that is going to initiate best practices, you can't be top-down driven. Not that I don't stay involved and want to stay involved, but you have to foster the ability for your junior leaders and your waiters and everybody to have their own sense of dominion over the place.

How do you foster that sense of dominion?

For example, I could have ordered everybody to do Schedulefly, but instead I just continued to bring it up and mention its advantages. And actually there was a waiter who was very familiar with it from his other job, and the combination of me saying it and that waiter saying it led to other waiters saying, "Hey, we need to try this out." And, boom, it gets done.

The key is, the best ideas come from our staff themselves. At the same time, it's tough to create an environment where good ideas bubble up but you don't get drowned by conflicting noise.

I understand that you have also done some unique things with your beverages.

Yes, we were the fourth brewery in the country to put our beer into a can. I perceived it originally as a way that my guests could walk out with a six pack, and have it better packaged than a growler, which is what we all do in the brew-pub world.

But even though I talked to the canning machine people for six months, they didn't tell me that I had to buy a minimum of 160,000 cans. So suddenly I was forced to try to create a distribution business out of this beer. Surprisingly it was very successful. So successful in fact that I realized that I needed to be able to make more beer.

Ultimately all of that made me realize that I didn't want to be in the canned beer business at all, but rather I wanted to be in the micro-distilling business. So we're going to create the first vodka and gin distillery in the state of North Carolina, and we're very excited about that. I want to add a caveat — we're the first *legal* vodka and gin distillery in the state of North Carolina. [Laughs]

You opened a second location in Raleigh at one point, and then closed it a couple of years later. Why?

Actually, in many ways, that was one of the most important things I ever did. I realized that I had excess beer, and I was looking for another way to use that beer. So my thought process was to go ahead and start another restaurant.

That experience helped me realize that my passion was not the restaurant business per se, but it was the Chapel Hill business. I realized that I love Chapel Hill, and being in the restaurant business is what allows me to be in Chapel Hill. Consequently, that enabled me to focus lots of decisions, because I realized that I was splitting my energy between two stores.

By the way, God bless an independent that can run two or three stores. I'm told that once you get to five it gets easier, but I'm telling you, having two or three is a bear.

I realized that I could take half the energy I was putting into the new store and make more money. I took a look at the very best amount of money I could make in Raleigh, and realized that it was the equivalent of 5% of my sales here in Chapel Hill. So I asked myself, "If I focus all of my attention on Chapel Hill, can't I run it 5% better?"

Sure enough, we combined teams, and got rid of some folks that were not necessarily at the top of their game, and we came back in and rejuvenated the menu here in Chapel Hill, and ultimately ended up cutting overhead costs by 12%. I was suddenly making twice as much money, and working half as much. That was nice. [Laughs] And it allowed me to indulge in my passion, which was downtown Chapel Hill itself.

Consequently, understanding that has shaped my business decisions since then. Everything from the decision to be involved with the business school as an adjunct professor, to starting the distillery, because the distillery is downtown as well.

The way I look at that is, "Yes, we're in the distribution business, but what I am exporting is Chapel Hill." I think the distillery is going to add a lot of excitement and coolness to our downtown, and it reinforces the existing brand.

Also, that extra energy was turned into doing the expansion. Now we're about a 22,000 square-foot facility. So being able to focus on expanding what we have, rather than opening another location, has allowed us to really harness our energy in a synergetic way.

I would caution folks to really consider carefully whether you want to expand to another town, or whether you even want to expand at all. Any expansion – even though we feel really comfortable with what we've done – brings lots of challenges. You have to spend a lot of time creating a successful restaurant, and doubling it doesn't necessarily mean that it's going to make you any more money.

Parting thoughts?

Going back to the idea of the business plan, and the idea the independent has only got "weird and whacky" left. The other thing that the independent has that no amount of money can replace, is the true understanding of the local community. A well-funded chain restaurant can blow an independent away with restaurant design, menu design and all of that stuff (if they chose to, and there is enough capital behind it).

But the problem is that, by its definition, to justify that type of capital expense it needs to be replicatable, and that is the chains' Achilles' heel. What the money can't do, is it can't drill down into one community and understand what that community needs. Chains can't do that. An independent can.

Highlights – A recap of Scott's key points...

- ✓ Lack of intimate local knowledge is the Achilles' heel of chains

- ✓ If you plan to raise money, start your pitch with your last prospects

- ✓ You're not a restaurateur – you're a business person

- ✓ Foster autonomy with your staff

- ✓ Do more with one location vs. opening a second location

Simplicity, catches
& the importance of hiring sales people
for every position

Bub's Burgers & Ice Cream
Bub's Café
150+ employees
Carmel, IN
Bloomington, IN
Restaurant owner since 2003
www.bubsburgersandicecream.com

Matt left a career in corporate sales to open Bub's with his wife, Rachel. Both had worked in restaurants, but had never owned one or even managed one. Seven years later, Bub's was featured on the hit Food Channel show, "Man v. Food." Like any successful entrepreneur, Matt had the attitude that failure was not an option and he's built a successful business around that mentality. In fact, he said several

*times that he looks at Bub's as a business, not a restaurant. Matt had
many inspiring and educational things to say about everything from
keeping a concept simple, to having a catch to draw people in, to
hiring sales people for every position at Bub's...*

Tell me how you got started in the restaurant business.

At age 14, I was cleaning dishes over at a banquet facility that my
brother-in-law and sister had opened back in '85 here in Carmel,
Indiana. It was a breaking point for that industry because back then,
downtown Indianapolis was the only place you would really go do
weddings, receptions and other events. He and my sister Lynn were
visionaries to open their own banquet facility north of Indianapolis in
Carmel, Indiana. I owe them a large part of my success.

After college, I worked as a food broker for a couple of years and also
at Kellogg Food Services. I got to know the networks of the
distributors, the distribution business, the brokerage business and
the manufacturing business. I traveled extensively for a number of
years and I eventually got tired of being on the road. That's when I
talked to my brother-in-law, who said, "Do your own restaurant."

I knew it would be a big step. It's hard to leave that comfort zone
with a 401(k), the company car, the insurance, the benefits and all
the trips they were taking me on. Then I thought, "You know what?
You live once and you can try it, and if it doesn't work I can always go
back to sales."

I sat down with Rachel and I said, "Let's think about a restaurant."
She said, "Nahhh...no way." She was unfamiliar with the food
business, so it was a big thing. It was a big step, a big risk. But you
live once, you keep your fingers crossed, and if you work hard, things
will turn out okay.

How were you able to make it work?

I think what makes us stand apart is the way we operate the business. I think that's the key – it's a business, not a restaurant.

Also, I had that experience of knowing distribution, manufacturers and pricing, which is crucial to any success in business. You've got to be good at buying to succeed. A lot of people get into this, and then leave to go into that manufacturing side, the brokerage side or the distribution side, because owning and operating a restaurant became too hard.

Tell me about the business plan that you put together.

The business plan was the concept of having a burger shop and having a catch called the "Big Ugly® burger." It's a business, and you need a marketing campaign. You need something to draw people in besides just throwing a sign on a wall or the door and saying, "Yeah, we sell food."

You want to make people desire to come in. You can't just have a burger shop. You just can't have a steak house. When you walk in the front door of Bub's, you see a display case like a butcher shop, and the Big Ugly® is pre-pattied out. It's sitting there with the bun that comes with it, and then there's the Not So Ugly®, the Settle for Less® and the Mini Bub®.

It's that little catch that gets people to come in. They wonder, "What's the Big Ugly®?"

I guess you have a point. The Big Ugly Burger caught the attention of the hit TV show called "Man v. Food." They featured Bub's in a recent episode.

Yes, and now all of a sudden we've got national and basically worldwide freakin' advertising on it. We've had people come in from Ireland, London, you name it. Some guy called me and said, "How do I get there?" I said, "Well, I need to know where you're coming from." The guy replied, "Arkansas!" I said, "Really?!" He said, "Hell yes! It looks so good on TV, we're coming up and bringing the family." I'm thinking, "Are you out of your mind?"

To get that kind of exposure is just priceless. I mean, it's comical. During a busy summer week, we'd sell about 190 Big Uglies before the show aired. The week after it aired, we sold 672. The second week it aired we sold over 700. It's maintained at the 400 or 500 level since the show aired. [The show aired in August, 2010. This interview was conducted in early January, 2011] Just this past week we were so busy we sold 629.

How much time did you spend planning the restaurant?

I met with the mayor two years before we opened because I originally wanted to buy or lease a property in the downtown area that the city owned. I said, "Look, I've grown up in Carmel, so I've gotten a lot out of the city and I want to give something back, something I think it lacks."

At that time we had a major influx of chain restaurants moving into town. I wanted to put up a family restaurant that had great food and great service, but also was unique in terms of doing one or two things very well.

So it was important to keep your concept simple?

I can tell you that's a large part of why restaurants fail. They get into the business and all of a sudden they've got everything from fish, chicken, beef, pork chops. You just flip through the menu and you're asking yourself, "What the hell do I want?"

When you come to Bub's, you know what you're going to get. If you're good at one or two things, and continue to focus on service and cleanliness, you'll set yourself up for success.

How did you finance it?

The first bank I went to said no about three times, and I wouldn't take that. The guy eventually said yes, and then I had a five-year loan, which I paid back in two years. That about knocked them out of their boots because it's just one of those things – you have to have that attitude of saying that failure is not even close to being an option. It's amazing how your body and your mind will respond if you think that way.

What's your advice for people planning to borrow money?

You have to have skin in the game. Count on having at least 20% down. There's no bank out there that's going to say, "Okay, you need $250,000, here's the full $250,000." Instead, you'll hear, "We'll give you $200,000. You've got to have $50,000 down at least." And you've got to have some cash leftover.

Also, I went to one local bank because I knew I'd speak to somebody that would have a little bit more of an understanding of our goal and our mission, and also a little bit more flexibility compared to a large bank.

Why did you pay back your loan in two years?

There were a few reasons. The interest scare, the pride factor and the need to prove them wrong. The first couple tries they said no, I was thinking, "This is going to work whether you think so or not."

I don't like to get told no. I remember telling the bank, "You're going to loan me this money, I'm going to pay you back, and I'm going to show you that you're wrong." You have to have a winning attitude at all times.

I'm a firm believer that it's what you say, but also more importantly it's how you say it in life. I teach my staff that as well. But I had more willingness to do it because of pride and being able to say, "Look, you're wrong."

I think the restaurant business has a very bad reputation – burnouts, losers, divorcées, whatever. I refuse to settle for that mediocrity and that kind of attitude. It can be done right.

You focus a lot on the importance of sales.

You bet. When I hire, it's salespeople and not waiters. I think that's what every restaurant owner should focus on. Anyone can go, "Hi, my name is Ashley. What do you want to eat today?" The first thing you say is, "Hi, how are you?" You create a relationship and you talk about the menu, and you talk about the promotions, or the soup of the day and carry on to close the deal.

How important is it to have the right kind of staff in your restaurant?

It's absolutely vital. They're a complete reflection of me and my family.

It's well known at this point what to expect when they walk in. They know that we hire young people. I'm very active in the marketing classes and entrepreneur classes at the local high school, talking about sales and how important it is any business, not just at Bub's. I tell them we don't hire ice cream scoopers, bussers, dishwasher, hosts or waiters. We hire salespeople.

If we hire you to dish, if you're content with that, you'll last about a week here. You should be motivated enough to say, "Okay, what do I have to do here to get my feet on that floor to make that cash?" We hire 15-year-olds. Those kids walk out with $100 - $150 bucks cash in their pockets after working four hours. These are the kids that gave you that goofy look when you spoke about ROI and maximizing profitability, but when they walk out with that cash, they fully understand and they take it seriously after that.

How do you find people that you can trust and that share your same belief and passion?

It really comes down to word of mouth. I've tried other things like Monster.com, but I've had better success with talking to people I know. That's so important.

When you find one or two good kids that work hard, they hang with that same type of personality. So if you find one, they've typically got one or two more. Once you get your foot in with one or two kids who understand what you're doing and start making money, their friends are pretty jealous and they want a part of that.

People must line up hoping to work for you.

I've got a reputation in town of not being the easiest guy to work for, but I have people that have been with me eight years, seven years, six years, five years. They believe in it. That's the pride in ownership. I've succeeded if I can get these people to truly understand sales when they leave us and graduate from college, or move on from one corporate job to another and they're doing this part time. Maybe they'll look back and say, "Yes, he was a complete ass to work for, but he was right. This is what it takes."

I'm not one to say that I know everything or I'm the best at what I do or all this kind of crap, but it's almost like being a teacher. If you reach one or two kids out there, they're going to be better parents, better spouses, better friends. And they'll have a little better understanding of what it takes to be a team player: work hard, be trustworthy, be honest, exceed expectations and understand that you are always measured based on your performance.

How does turnover impact you?

The turnover rate for us is really hard. Like I said, we're busiest in the summer, so we have 90 people on payroll here in Carmel. And that's just the burger shop. Then everyone goes back to school, and you drop down from 90 to maybe 30, so it's a constant training cycle.

That's why those sales meetings every two weeks come in handy.

What do you talk about in those meetings?

We talk about service. We ask them where they went out to eat, and whether they observed anything that made them think about their own service at our restaurant. "Did the waiter talk to you, or did you just let him take your order?"

They all come back to me and say, "Thanks a lot. I can't even go out to eat anymore because I see everything. You would have died if you would have seen this." And we talk about that, and our customers see it when we wait tables and all those things that go into it. We constantly train about proper service techniques, constant live questions about our own menu. Knowledge is power.

How is your business faring in this tough economic environment?

Actually I've seen in the news that Carmel, IN., is one of the cities in the country that's kind of protected against this recession environment. But at the same time, our business model helps as well. Our average tab per person might be $11, whereas the finer dining establishments are taking more of a hit.

We're staying focused, we're a fun place, and our staff is all part of that equation. It's so important to hire the right people because they've got to buy into it as well.

What types of technology help you run your business?

I'm 39, but I'm kind of old school when it comes to twittering and Facebooking. There are so many different avenues to reach customers and to reach the staff.

I can tell you that Schedulefly has been tremendously helpful. Stuff always comes up, and I think that the ease of communication from employee to employee is tremendously helpful. Eight years ago, I was on our Excel spreadsheet doing the schedule, trying to interpret handwritten notes from our employees. Good God, man, what a nightmare!

The staff really enjoys it too because it's almost like Facebook. It's shared, it has their picture, it enables them to post notes or requests – or whatever else – so I think they get a kick out of it too. And I think the fact that we're willing to invest in something like this shows them that we're serious, and they buy into that as well.

What else do you think has made you successful in an industry that has such a high failure rate?

There's no way I could just do this alone. My wife, Rachel, is critical.

I think the largest part of failure rates in restaurants is people get in and they all of a sudden think that they're an accountant or a bookkeeper or an IT person.

I'm definitely front of the house, and Rachel's back of the house. She can sit in front of a computer all day long. She can analyze, she can do all that stuff that I just can't do. I can't stand it. I've got to be on my feet moving around, where she's fine with that stuff.

One of the best decisions she and I made when we first started was we hired an accountant, and we had a bookkeeper to keep us straight and keep us focused. I think a lot of restaurants do it all themselves. There are a lot of tools out there that enable you to afford to do it on your own, but I think it's too hard. There's too much going on. It's worth the expense to outsource that stuff to somebody that you completely trust. I think that was one the great decisions that we made.

Again, just going down into it, first you have the menu, being good at one or two things, having a good location and a fun environment and training the staff so they truly understand what they're supposed to accomplish – it's all part of the gig.

How do you manage growth?

The hardest part about growth is not just that you can't be two places at once, but that you lose that contact with the customers you've seen several times a week for the past few years. If you want to grow you have to let go and surround yourself with people you trust, and know that they have the same philosophy you have in the business.

If you can do that you're going to be able to go to each location, spend a day or two at each one, and motivate and do other things.

What's your plan for future growth?

A large reason restaurants fail is greed and ego. So when the time is right, we'll grow more. When the time is right we'll franchise or build more units.

We get a lot of requests for franchises right now. After "Man v. Food" aired, a lawyer from Atlanta called. He represents clients in London and South Korea that might put a burger concept in those locations. And they want us.

The guy came to Carmel, loved the product, brought some people with him, and just went nuts over it. But you know what, I don't know who this guy is, and I'll be damned if I'm going to do business with somebody I don't know. He's having a hard time understanding that. But the only people in my business right now are me and Rachel, and that's the way we'd like to keep it for awhile.

But who knows? Nobody opens a business, works seven days a week, 15-hour days. You open a business, you grow it and then sell it. So who knows what will happen?

You mentioned greed and ego contribute to restaurant failures. Why?

If anyone tells you they don't like the recognition, they're lying. You want to be recognized for the hard work that you've done. To what extent, that's up to you. Everybody likes that recognition, but some people desire it way too much.

Some people really need it to live, but I don't. I'm working hard and I love going home and saying, "Yeah, I earned my money today." Some people grow to increase their fame. They'll be blessed with a really great first year and then all of sudden they make a place twice as big and twice as expensive. The next thing you know they have twice the headaches and they're out of business.

So you've really got to be pretty subtle and humble in this business, because it can go pretty quickly from you. How you manage success really determines the type of person you are, in my opinion.

Do you run a lean operation?

Yeah, sure do. Labor costs, food costs. Both are critical. If you create a restaurant, keep it simple so you have little to no waste. You can use products in different ways. For example, bacon – it's on two or three menu items here, which is pretty common sense.

What else is working for you Matt?

We're a family business. The customers know me and my wife. They've seen my kids grow up. And one of the coolest things is that we'll be eight years old in May, and these young couples that came in when they just moved here, just when we first opened, were pregnant with their first child or second kids.

Now these kids are seven and eight years old, and they're coming in and they give us hugs. That's the hardest thing with the expansion too is that I'm not here to see them as much.

The biggest thing that I think these restaurant owners should look forward to is those relationships you have with your customers down the road. That's what you should strive for. Not the money, not the notoriety or anything like that.

Your biggest advantage over a chain restaurant is that people know who you are and they understand what you're trying to accomplish. If you work hard and be honest, it really will pay off.

Another owner told me the Achilles' heel for chains was not being able to have the intimate, local knowledge and connection to the community that you have when you're independent.

Yeah, and that's what you really have to consider when franchising or expanding. What maturity level is your business at? You might say, "Screw it. Screw all those relations with those people. Now it's about the money."

So what's the goal of the business? You really have to ask those things yourself. That's where you decide, "Okay, I'm content doing what I'm doing and I'm not going to grow." Or you say, "This is a business and we're going to grow it and we'll sell it and live happily ever after." Or you say, "I'm going to continue to work hard for the next 20 to 30 years, hand this over to my kids and just be content."

You really need to decide. And it's hard for us, I guess sometimes, with the popularity of it. There are a lot of pressures that go along with this. It's pretty amazing. More than I ever thought it would be.

Highlights – A quick recap of Matt's key points...

- ✓ It's a business, not a restaurant

- ✓ You have to have the attitude that failure is not an option

- ✓ You need a catch to draw people in

- ✓ Keep your concept simple

- ✓ Hire sales people for every position

- ✓ If you want to grow, you have to let go

Homework, hiring good people
& focusing on what's happening inside
your four walls

A Good Egg Dining Group
300+ employees
Oklahoma City, OK
Restaurant owner since 2000
www.goodeggdining.com

Keith Paul and his wife, Heather, opened their first restaurant in 2000. Now they own A Good Egg Dining Group, which has six extremely successful and popular restaurants (Cheever's Cafe, Iron Starr Urban BBQ, Red PrimeSteak, Market-C, Republic Gastropub, Pops) and a catering business (Cheever's Catering). Keith came from the food distribution business, having worked at Ben E. Keith Foods for a number of years. He has learned to keep it simple, do his homework and focus his attention on what's happening between the four walls of his restaurants. Six successful restaurants in 10 years? Pay attention to what Keith has to say...

How did you get started in the restaurant business?

My background is foodservice distribution. I was with a regional company, Ben E. Keith Foods, for 11 years in Ft. Worth, TX and Oklahoma City. When I moved up here in '95, I met Heather, who was also working for Ben E. Keith.

Heather's mother was involved in a couple of restaurants when she was growing up, and I had only worked in one restaurant in my life before jumping out and doing the Cheever's thing. Cheever's was a restaurant before we bought it. It was a customer of mine, and the previous owner was just ready to get out, so it was a good opportunity.

We both wanted to do something else, so we bought Cheever's as is, and the property came along with it. So that was really the only way that we were able to do anything. Money was just hard to come by, especially for somebody with zero experience. Not only zero experience in the restaurant business, but zero experience raising money in general.

Heather worked for two years, and every dime I made at Ben E. Keith, after paying personal bills, went back into the business. We finally turned a little profit, and that's when I started cooking. I worked at Ben E. Keith during the day and cooked at night for about 12 months to 18 months.

What prompted you and Heather to go out on your own after many years working for somebody else? That's a risky proposition.

Well, it was a huge risk. Heather really wanted to do something different, or something on her own, and I've always wanted to do something on my own. But it was a huge risk.

Ben E. Keith foods is one of the top foodservice firms in the country, if not the top. So I really had a good spot to stay in. I would have been fine, and we would have been doing great. But it was just intriguing to think of doing it on our own.

The building that Cheever's is in was built in 1904, so there were a lot of different factors in play. If someone was going to come sell the idea to us, we would have jumped on it immediately, because it had everything we really liked about the idea. The old building. The restaurant in general. The size of the restaurant.

Being on the distribution side, both of us were in kitchens of some of the nicest restaurants and most successful restaurants in the city. We saw the good, the bad and the ugly. We took all of that, and filtered it, and this is what we came up with. So there was never any doubt. Once the previous owner approached us, it was full steam ahead.

Did you take on debt to buy Cheever's?

Yes. We got a mortgage for the property. It was a relationship thing, because we knew the banker in town at the time. Also, times were pretty good here in Oklahoma City in April of 2000.

We tried to raise money from just family and friends. Friends were saying, "No." So it was really my parents and Heather's parents at the time who kind of kicked in a little cash, to give us a down payment for the bank. It was probably the most risky thing that my parents or her parents have ever done.

Were there times when you had doubts and were worried that you may have made a wrong decision?

Yeah, probably every month for 18 months. Like I said, every paycheck I got from Ben E. Keith paid personal bills, and the rest went back into the business. We were slow paying some vendors. It was scary at times. Heather was the GM, working 80 hours a week, 100 hours a week sometimes.

What were you focused on when you started?

We concentrated on what was happening inside the four walls of the restaurant, and on making sure every customer had a good time. And we were putting out a great product. We never skimped on quality. We never skimped on employee satisfaction – which I think is probably our main strength.

As we grew, we said "Let's make sure that everybody that works for us is completely happy. We'll do what we can for them. We're going to take a vested interest in their personal lives, and we're not going to spend a bunch of money on traditional advertising. We're not going to buy newspaper and radio and TV ads. We're gonna just concentrate on what's going on inside the four walls."

We kept attracting great people, and our culture has always been to keep our employees happy. And never, ever – even if times are slow – we never even think about skimping on quality of food, of silverware, of glassware, or anything. We've always stuck to those values and principles, and that has seemed to pay off.

Iron Starr was the first time you opened a second location for one of your concepts?

Yes, and we found that it's a lot easier to open up a second location for an existing concept than it is to start another brand new concept. Your systems are totally different with a new one, and so on.

However, the next place we opened was Republic Gastropub, which is our take on the gastro pub. Huge TVs. 100 beers on tap. 250 by the bottle.

Why has it all worked so well for you?

With all of these restaurants, we've just always gone back to that employee thing. We keep our people happy, and we recruit and hire great people. For instance, we couldn't have done Republic without hiring a beverage person. The guy we hired had 10 years of experience working for a large liquor distributor here in town.

Things like that have really helped us continue to grow. Are we trying to be the biggest? No, we're not. But why just sit back and let your ideas go to waste? We have tons of great ideas. Some maybe aren't so great, but we think they are. Maybe they will work, maybe they won't work. But we keep a lot of things in mind while we're talking about our growth.

For instance, we have close to 300 employees now that are kind of dependent on us to not make a bad decision. We don't go into it with a lot of fear involved, but we've just got to be cautious of a lot of different things.

We think only one of our restaurants is in a good location. So that's kind of a good and a bad thing. We think we can go into a good location now, and we think the odds of failure are less than 5%.

It's been a lot of fun. We've really built some great partnerships with our suppliers. We don't beat our suppliers up on price. We spend our time doing other things to try to promote our business, and just try to do the right thing.

Your website mentions core values of "creativity, teamwork and giving fulfilling career opportunities to team members." What do you mean by creativity?

We encourage everybody to be themselves. We want their individual personalities to come out. Anybody that wants to speak up, we encourage it, just promote that creativity. We want to hear ideas from dishwashers, from servers, chefs, cooks, managers, partners. We want to hear it all, because we don't know everything.

We started out as a one-unit, independent restaurant. Even if we had 50 restaurants, we don't want that corporate feeling. Even though, behind the scenes, on the systems part of it, we have taken on some of those successful corporate traits that really help run the business.

Tell me about "teamwork and providing fulfilling career opportunities."

As far as career opportunities, we do our best to promote from within. That goes back to just listening to our employees. We try to be in the stores as much as we can, and we want them to tell us what they want to do with their lives. We want them to tell us that, yeah, they're in school now, and their degree is in education. However, when they graduate they'd love to move from Cheever's over to Red PrimeSteak and learn more about wine, and possibly take their Sommelier test.

If someone comes to us and wants to travel, and go to seminars, and do all of these things, we encourage that. We want people to explain why they want to do it, and what's in it for them, what's in it for us. We know all of these things, but we want to make sure they know it, and can see the educational advantages. And if so, we're definitely going to pay for it.

And the teamwork thing really starts at the top with us. We need everybody involved to be successful, and we do our best to get that message across. We have roundtable meetings at the restaurants, with servers, with the kitchen, and so forth, and they tell us what will make their restaurant better. If they tell us they all need to come in 15 minutes early to get their shift duties and opening duties done, and that it will help the guest experience, then they've got our support, so that whole thing just comes together. We'll pick up those ideas and incorporate them throughout our group.

You don't do much traditional marketing, but rather focus on what's happening between the four walls. Are you creating awareness through word of mouth?

Yes, and it does take longer. However, we know that the chances of success are very high by following that path. You have a very small chance of failure there, if you're doing everything right, and you're putting your effort into the project, instead of writing checks to different media outlets, which is un-measurable.

When we were starting out with Cheever's and Iron Starr, we didn't have the money to do any advertising. So that's about 50% of the reason that we didn't do it. The other half of that comes from what I learned from being on the distribution side. It's almost impossible to advertize or promote for one unit, or even two units. I didn't believe in spending money on TV, radio, or newspaper that would reach people that were 50 miles away from me. I'm actually paying for that, but those people aren't going to come visit my restaurant. I knew that the core customers were within a five to 10 mile radius, max. So I wasn't going to do that traditional stuff.

But I'll tell you what, we did make a few mistakes. Once we had some money, we did experiment with some different magazines — different local publications. We did that on and off for about three years. And right now, with social media, I'm gradually scaling back. We've hired a communications director, and I would rather spend the money on this person than I would that traditional advertising. We've been doing that for about six months, and we feel it's paid off tremendously.

What types of things is she doing?

Communications director means just what it says. It's communications within our office, and every restaurant, and within the community. So any time someone is talking, she's kind of our go-to person. She's keeping our restaurant group on the tip of everyone's tongue in the community. We're getting involved in a lot more things than we ever have been. We're not spending money on newspapers and things like that. We're spending money on her salary, and she's creating opportunities. Things like having us show up at fundraisers, and getting different groups in the restaurant.

We've always been a firm believer that if we can get people in the restaurant, then we've got 'em as a customer. We could get 100 people into one of our restaurants, and we might keep 90 as a customer.

What kind of people do you hire?

Being a good person — that's really what we look for. We don't necessarily look for people with tons of restaurant experience. We think if they're a good person and they're great at what they do, then they'll be great here. If they're the best lawn mower in the country, then they're going to be good at whatever they do, so we get them in our group, and we can work with them, and kind of find their place.

And it's not just an overnight deal. We've come to find out that it just doesn't happen by sitting down with someone, and just talking about how their day was, or how school has been, or what their career goals are, or their kids and their soccer team. It's just the entire process that lasts forever. At some point you start to see results, and it makes it all worth it. You know you're doing things right. But that might be the hardest thing to explain of anything we do.

You look back 20 years ago at the restaurant business, and you had chefs throwing pans across the kitchen. You had restaurant owners talking to employees like they weren't human. There was something in the restaurant industry — some kind of stigma that still goes on — that they want to work you 80 hours a week every single week, and this business is just night and day. And there's no way you can have a personal life with it.

Our deal is, we want you to work five days a week, 50 hours a week. Sometimes 60 hours during holidays and busy times. But that's your average. On your day off, we don't want you coming around. Right when we hire somebody, we tell them, "Your family comes first, and we'd love to be second."

What have you learned over the years that has surprised you?

What I've been surprised about is that having one unit is very difficult. Having two makes it twice as much work. But as you get to three, to four, to five, we found it to be easier to control. I think it's opened up some doors, as far as accounting and things like that, to do things in-house. That's not a very sexy answer, I guess. [Laughs] But that's what I have seen.

The other part – not that it surprised me, because I've seen it during my 11 years of the distribution side – is that I've seen restaurants go out of business because a one-unit guy opens up another one, and then all of a sudden, instead of one losing money, now you have two losing money. So he goes and opens up another one, and the third one supports the other two, and all of a sudden you go out of business. I've seen that a lot on the distribution side of it.

I get this question all of the time: "Are you just working your butt off all of the time now?" I'm not. I'm actually working less than I did when we had one. I think it's a credit to the way we hired people, and the people we put in place. I'm often criticized by everybody around here about how we spend so much money on salaries, and how we have too many people. But those feelings go away after I explain to them that a lot of people that we have are specialized at what they do, so it's taken a lot of workload off of what we're all doing. They're great at their particular profession, so it's really an advantage to the entire group for us to have these people on staff. We're probably a little top heavy, and that's probably just how it will always be.

Does that mean that you save a lot of money by having lower turnover as well?

Exactly. I think turnover is just a killer. I hate it more than anything. And I've seen it with one of our restaurants. We get reports every week about prime cost, and the way the performance of the restaurant is going. About a year ago, I would always get a comment such as, "We're still training. We're training this person. The front of the house is training this person." And that's not an excuse of why the labor cost is high. It's the direct result of too much turnover. So now we've stopped the turnover, and there's three or four extra points on the bottom line because of that.

So, yeah, that's a big deal to me. I just hate turnover.

Why do so many restaurants fail in the first three to five years?

I think it's a combination of things. Number one is not doing their homework, and not doing their homework causes these other components to arise. Meaning, they don't have enough operating cash, because they think they're going to make money right off the bat.

Or they don't have the extra pieces, like lease negotiation. We didn't know a thing about that when we were getting into it. And that's huge. If you don't have the right lease going in, and you have an air conditioner that goes down in your first month, then you're out $8,000 - $10,000.

There are just so many things, and it all really goes back to not doing your homework. Not reading personal stories like you're putting into this book. Or just keeping up with trends, and eating out. There are so many restaurateurs and chefs around the country that don't eat at the competition. I just don't get that. At all. I don't understand it one bit. It's all homework.

I actually talked to a guy the other day who wanted to open a bar here in town that also served food. I just kinda told him, "The bottom line is, you shouldn't do it. You're coming to me with nothing. You don't have a clear concept." It's another homework thing. Lack of a clear concept and operating cash are two things that can arise that can really kill a new venture like that.

What are your plans for the future?

We think we've got a couple of ideas up our sleeve ... a couple of new concepts that can be fun and that Oklahoma City needs. The city in general is bouncing back from this recession favorably compared to other markets. So we're going to sit tight for the next six months, and then we'll probably do two more units next year – late next year – and we'll just see what happens after that.

Highlights – A quick recap of Keith's key points...

✓ Focus on what's going on inside your four walls

✓ Learn from everybody on your team – you don't know it all

✓ Look for good people over experienced ones

✓ Be second to your staff's family

✓ Number two won't balance a failing number one

✓ Being top heavy is O.K. if you've got great people

Accounting, partnerships
& how running a restaurant is an art,
not a science

Friends Coastal Restaurant
50+ employees
Madisonville, LA
Restaurant owner since 2004
www.friendscoastal.com

Friends Coastal Restaurant is a New Orleans-meets-Key West restaurant. It's the only business directly over the beautiful waters of Tchefuncta River in Madisonville, and it has seen an increase in sales, or the same sales, almost every month since it opened in 2006. Richard came from the IT world, and had no restaurant experience. He and his former partner split ways recently, but Richard and his new partner, Ryan Richard, have Friends trucking right along and doing great business. Richard has learned a lifetime of valuable lessons over the last four years, such as how critical it is to work with a quality CPA [certified public accountant], the dilemma of being leveraged and the importance of being consistent. Here's what he had to say about those issues and a few others...

Why did you get into the restaurant business?

I was in the IT world before I was a restaurant owner. One day, a childhood buddy, Chris, called me and said he had an idea for a restaurant concept, and asked for help with the business plan. He had been involved in the restaurant business all of his life. He had worked at a place in Madisonville called Friends for a few years when he was younger, and had kept in touch with the owners. It just so happened that as he was looking for locations, Hurricane Katrina hit, and the owners of Friends were interested in selling.

Chris presented his concept, and the owners liked it, and they worked out a lease-purchase option. Chris called me, and I thought it was a cool opportunity. I knew about Friends, and I knew the location was incredible. It's the only business directly on the Tchefuncta River, and that's grandfathered in. You can't build out on the river any longer.

The concept also made sense. It was a Key West-meets-New Orleans concept, and being on the water tied to the fact that both of those places are surrounded by water.

How did you fund the opening?

We went through the process of trying to raise some capital. The building was damaged by hurricane Katrina, to the extent that it needed about $500,000 dollars in renovations and repairs, to bring it up to what our concept was. So we raised about $200,000 to match the insurance money, and we had a little bit of extra money to get started with. All of the investment money came from family members.

We did a pro-forma to show what it would take for that place to stay in operation, and make a profit. We had great information, because we had all of the financials from the previous owners to help us gauge how many people would come through there, and things like that. So we had a really good basis for knowing what the restaurant was capable of. And we knew what areas of improvement we could do to generate more revenue, and what modifications we needed to make to accommodate those ideas.

You started out leveraged. How did that affect your decisions?

It's not something I would necessarily recommend to anybody. We had some other investors that were ready to back us up, but we started out leveraged. It makes you really conscious of exactly where your costs are, and your spending. If you don't absolutely need something, you don't buy it.

It leaves you vulnerable to not having the cash flow to get through some swings. We had some cash in the bank, but not enough to carry ourselves for a few months. In fact, if you start a restaurant, you should be able to carry yourself for a year, to go through your exposure and stuff like that.

We felt like we already had a lot of exposure. A restaurant had been there for 25 years. We're in a small community, and we were able to get the word out. So I wasn't nervous about being somewhat leveraged, but I wouldn't recommend it. It puts a financial stress on you when you dip through a slow week or whatever, and that takes its toll on you.

Fortunately, we came out of the gates with a bang. We had a lot of people that showed up for the first dry run, and after that, it was just steady as she goes.

How steady?

Prior to us being involved, the previous restaurant had done anywhere between $800,000 and just over $1,000,000 in sales per year. In our first year, we did $1,800,000. The next year was $2,100,000. Then $2,300,000. And last year we did $2,500,000.

What has helped you be successful?

First of all, we've maintained a good number of people that were here when we got started. We have an open-door policy, and we want to have a very good relationship with our staff. We genuinely care about them, and we try to have very open communication. Sometimes somebody might have lost a loved one, or maybe they run into financial problems. We're very open about trying to help people out when we can, and at least at giving them an ear. That's really worked well for us.

Also, after the first six months or so, we started working with a CPA. I highly, highly recommend hiring a CPA, especially one who is close to the restaurant industry. They understand what percentages should be, as an average. Without breaching confidentiality, they can talk to you about what other restaurants do to combat certain cost structures that you have. Our CPA, Patrick Gros, has been very instrumental in helping us cut costs, and in telling us what percentages should be. He recommends the financial applications that we should use, and helps us with reading P&L's [profit and loss reports], and how to make adjustments. And that's really helped us out quite a bit.

When you can work with CPAs on a daily basis, and have them help assure that budgets are aligned and cost controls are adhered to, it's just as important to me as the food you put on the plate. Without controlling those costs, you don't make money.

If you're in it just to make a paycheck, just do it on your own. Otherwise, I highly recommend you hire a CPA and make that a big part of your restaurant. Just as much as you would design a recipe for your food, you need to design a recipe for how you're going to track and adjust for financial costs and profits.

What else has worked?

We charted along for the first two or three years, and worked out the flow of everything. We worked out which vendors we use, and which ones we don't use, and we got to a point where we got comfortable enough lining up with certain vendors because we could lock in certain costs. And they give us a lot of kickbacks.

For example, with some of our liquor companies, if you buy a case, you get a couple of bottles for free. Things like that really help with your costs.

We've also learned to lean on our purveyors and vendors, to do things like give us menus if we give them a little advertising. That really cuts back costs. Once we realized they were willing to do that, and we had the volume to support it, we actually saved quite a bit of money on menus and specialty menus.

When we have big events they'll do a lot of signage, and have specials on their products, such as beer, alcohol and things like that.

When we do non-profit things, they're able to reduce the price even more.

These kinds of things can really help you in the beginning, because you don't have to do everything yourself. If you can't afford to do your own menu, or don't know how to put one together, or you don't know how to put a flyer or a banner together, it's going to cost you a lot of money to have somebody else to do it, or a lot of time out of running the operations of the business for you to do it. So, if you can lean on your vendors to do those kinds of things, it's going to save you a lot of time, and it doesn't cost you anything.

I'm not going to tell you that we've done everything right. We've certainly made some mistakes. But we try to learn from those mistakes, and listen to others who have been in this business, and utilize the knowledge of our CPA and our purveyors and vendors to try to streamline a lot of things.

What are you focused on now?

Now we're looking further into the details of things, and working off of half percentages, and percentages, to really fine tune things. We're bringing in technologies like Schedulefly, and FreshBooks [billing software], and Google email with calendaring. We're bringing in a lot of very inexpensive, but powerful, tools to help us keep all of our information together in a central location, and keep it secured. That has really helped our operations.

We're continuing to look at processes, and fine tuning them. We're looking at ways we can expand on our operations. If we get to a place where we feel that we can sew up our concept as a package, we may be able to implement it at other locations.

The ultimate goal is to have more than one Friends. It's a special location where it is now, and it would probably have to be a special location somewhere else. It really makes sense for our concept to be on the water, and to be in a place where it fits the scene.

You are very focused on the happiness and fulfillment of your staff. Is that one of the keys to restaurant success?

Yes. It is very key and vital to have a staff that is behind you and playing on the same team. I believe that's true in any business, but perhaps even more so in ours. If you have a very happy staff that is well-educated about your business, and their responsibilities and duties – and their compensation structure is right – then it will reflect on the customers.

I played football, so I see it like a football team. You have a coach, which is the owners. You have assistant coaches, which are the managers. You have the players, which are your staff.

You sell them on the plays that you're gonna run to win the game. Our plan is laid out, and we show them how we want it to be executed. Then we refine it and make adjustments as the plan is being executed.

It's vital to have a good relationship with your employees. But there is a fine line with not being too involved with them. You have to keep the relationship on a professional level. That doesn't mean that you can't be friends with them, but they have to understand that if you are friends, they can't get away with not fulfilling their responsibilities.

When you can balance it the right way, you have a really happy staff. They believe in you, and they want you to do well. I have employees tell me that they want us to make a lot of money. They want us to do extremely well, because they like who we are.

What food cost and labor cost percentages do you try to hit?

Well, I can tell you that we haven't always been successful at hitting the percentages we are looking for. Our typical labor and food costs are around 30%. Anything above 32% would be unacceptable. Our ideal situation is 28%, and definitely very doable for our organization. We have a couple of different tools that we use to look at where we are at any given time during the day, as far as percentage of labor. And based on what those percentages are, and based on other factors such as weather, and other events going on around the community, we can make adjustments.

It's been a very artful thing to try to do. You never know when you're just going to get pops of people. It's better to have more staff than you need, than less staff than you need, because you don't want to have a poor customer experience.

What keeps customers coming back?

I think our concept works really well in this community, and it's a very unique location. But I think what brings people back to Friends is that, while we've not always been 100% consistent with our food and service – and every restaurant battles with that – we try to improve on those things all of the time. I think we've gotten to a point where, when people come here, they know what to expect.

And what they should expect is great food and great service. The location is there, and the place is beautiful. So I think it's about executing those things, and because we have executed those things properly, we've built a relationship with our customers where they bring in their friends, and their family members, and it just grows from there. We've grown a customer base that counts on Friends as a consistent place to go.

You also have to account for the hurricanes that have come through here. We had Gustav and Ike. Before that, we had Katrina and Rita. Hurricanes do quite a bit to keep people home. People are more likely to be cautious and stay at home when they take time off. The storms hurt people financially, and maybe they don't have the funds to go anywhere.

Also, the slow economy has caused people to stay here as well. And then there's the disaster in the Gulf, with the oil spill. So they stay here, and do things like going out to Friends. The term "Staycation" is used often around here.

We've seen either the same sales, or an increase in sales, almost every month since we opened. That goes back to food quality, and presentation, and service.

Do you use social media tools to promote Friends?

Yes, social media certainly helps. We have over 800 fans on Facebook, and we just started using it a year ago. That number grows every week. It's free advertising. It's information that we dish out to our fan base on a daily basis. Our specials. Events that are coming up. It helps us with exposure, and helps us stay top of mind to all of those people as a destination and a place to go eat.

Chris recently exited the business. What have you learned from that departure?

I've learned that communication is very key to business partnerships. Everybody needs to be on the same page with executing the plan. Having meetings on a regular basis is important to know what issues you have and figure out how to address them.

With partnerships, you will sometimes run into situations where you have pressures financially, or personally, or something even outside of that. How everyone reacts to it, and deals with, determines the direction of how things go.

I've learned that you have to be very cautious about who you go into business with, and make sure that everybody is very aware of what the expectations are of the other partner. What involvement they will have. What everybody's compensation will be. What the boundaries are. And always, always put the business as number one. If you can do those things, you have a recipe for a very successful partnership.

We all hope that when you go into a partnership that it's going to be great. But it's like a marriage. You have to work on it. You can't just let things happen. You have to essentially be on the same page. You have to really think out the partnership as much as you do the plan for the business, because the issues and problems that arise from a bad partnership can cause the business to fail, and the friendship as well.

What have you learned over the years that you did not expect when you got started?

Every industry has its own personality. I had to learn the personality of the hospitality industry. It's filled with a lot of different artistic characters. I'm not saying that as a derogatory thing. It's just an adjustment I had to make to the types of personalities you find in this industry. I've played sports all of my life, and when you are on teams, you deal with lots of different personalities. So that helped me learn to make the adjustment.

I've also noticed that in this industry, more so perhaps than others, people who are promoted to management tend to have to be grounded if they haven't been in management before. It happens more than 50% of the time. They take it as if they have the power to do anything they want, and they take it to the extreme. In a lot of cases, it actually changes their personality. Even though you ask them to quietly go into their responsibilities, and treat people with respect, a lot of people just take it to the extreme.

That has surprised me. I feel like we've tried to do the proper due diligence before making those promotions, but I've been surprised more often than not on how people have adjusted. [Laughs] So we've had to make adjustments along the way.

The hospitality industry has a lot to do with perception. Little things mean a lot. How you maintain your facilities. Your bathrooms. Your baseboards. Your floors. Your walls. These things have nothing to do with the plate on the table. But they have everything to do with people's perception of your place, and how it's taken care of. You can say that about any business. But when you're working around food and perishables, keeping a clean place is something that needs to be taken to very seriously. Pay attention to the little things, because in the overall scheme of things, they are very large things.

Highlights – A few of Richard's key points...

✓ Have the cash to carry yourself for one year

✓ Take great care of your staff, and they'll help you succeed

✓ A good CPA is as important as good food

✓ Negotiate win-win deals with your vendors

✓ Technology will help you tighten things up

✓ Hitting labor cost targets is an art, not a science

✓ Be consistent and they will come

✓ Partnerships are like marriages

Edgy marketing, wagon wheels
& the view from 30,000 feet

Parasole Restaurant Group
1200+ employees
Minneapolis, MN
Restaurant owner since 1977
www.parasole.com

Phil Roberts is a legend in the restaurant business, having launched over a dozen successful restaurants, including Buca di Beppo and The Oceanaire Seafood Room, which both went public. He owns Parasole Restaurant Group, which has 10 extremely successful restaurants (Mozza Mia, Pittsburgh Blue, Il Gatto, Burger Jones, Manny's Steakhouse, Chino Latino, Uptown Cafeteria, Muffuletta, Salut, and Good Earth). Phil is bold, innovative, and knows what people want before they do. He's refreshingly unafraid to offer very honest opinions on any topic. Enjoy some great advice from a man who has proven himself over and over...

Thirty years ago you were a commercial designer traveling a lot from your home in Minneapolis to New York for business. Why did you decide to leave that profession and get into the restaurant business?

My clients were in New York and I was traveling there every other week, and my clients knew I was a foodie. They took pity on the poor little guy from Minnesota flyover country that had no culinary life. They took me to the best restaurants and to the newest and hottest things that New York had to offer. Every night we'd go out to a different place that was probably being reviewed in the New York Times that week. Then I'd come back to Minnesota to meat and potatoes. Pretty good meat and potatoes. But still – meat and potatoes. And, good Lord, I'd just had fettuccini alfredo. Or I'd just had quiche lorraine. Or I'd just had something I'd never heard of.

So that was what got me interested – I was traveling a lot, and seeing lots of things, and I was thinking, "I bet Minnesota could use something like this."

What happened next?

I enjoyed my business, but the travel was a killer. I had three little kids at home, and they were growing up while their dad was away. At that same time I kind of decided that I could do design work about as well as I ever cared to. I didn't care to learn the last 2% or 3% percent of the profession. I had already conquered 97% or 98% of it. So I thought, at that time in my life – I was probably 38, 39 years old – it's time to try something else. So I had a good friend whom I had known since college, and he and I bought this little neighborhood joint to try out some of our ideas. And it worked.

Did you do it with your own money?

Yes, we did it with our own money. It wasn't too terribly expensive, but it did deplete both of our savings. We had to refinance our houses and stuff. And with three kids – and he had six kids I think at the time – that's a hell of a time to bet the farm. But frankly that's what we did. And we started this little place called Muffuletta, and last year it had its best year ever, and it's been in business for 33 years now.

Did you put together a sound business plan?

Oh hell no! I started a company called The Oceanaire Seafood Room, which I left about five years ago. But one of the big steakhouse chains was interested in picking up Oceanaire, and I was sitting with the CEO at lunch one day, and he asked, "O.K. Roberts, what's your strategy for location for these Oceanaire Seafood rooms?" I said, "Well you show me a Morton's that's doing about $7,000,000. And you show me a Ruth's Chris that's doing about $7,000,000. I'll put The Oceanaire down right between the two of them and create the ultimate surf and turf." He asked, "That's your location strategy?" I said, "You're damn right it is. That's all I need."

So you use a lot of gut instinct to make decisions?

I'll tell ya, I've been in this business long enough. I have traveled hundreds of thousands of miles every year. And whether it's Europe, South Africa, Asia, New York, L.A., Houston – wherever. You gather

96

so much knowledge and information – you see so much of what is going on – that I am at the point in my career that, give me 10% of the information and I will make a decision. I let my instincts take over the other 90%.

It's good to have those kinds of instincts! Take me back to opening Muffuletta. You were getting into a completely new and risky business. What did you focus on to make it work?

I always view a restaurant sort of like a pie chart or a wagon wheel with lots and lots of spokes. Four or five of the spokes are food. Three or four are service. Some of them are ambience. Some are lighting. Some are uniforms. Some are the menu or the tone. It's very much like staging a Broadway play. The script is the menu. You've got the set design. You've got the music. You've got the lines. And it all has to deliver as a whole, and not as a bunch of parts. You can't get a couple of parts right and have it succeed. It's got to succeed as a whole.

You focus on where you want to be in that fine-dining spectrum. You've got everything from a QSR [quick service restaurant] at the bottom to Alain Ducasse au Plaza Athenee in Paris. And somewhere along that line you're going to pin the tail on the donkey. And you've got to decide just what level you want to be at. You want to avoid being too fancy in certain locations. You want to be the place where folks can come to fuel up, or have it be the main event. You want to focus on limiting your menu so you're not trying to do a hundred things like The Cheesecake Factory. You want to be able to take it to a dozen things and do them really well. Consistently.

You also started Buca di Beppo. Talk about that.

Yep, I started that in 1993. Buca wasn't particularly creative. Buca was just simple logic – getting up at 30,000 feet and looking down at what was going on. What I observed was that after World War II, you had about 25,000,000 immigrants come over from southern Italy and Sicily to this country, and a lot of them started mom-'n-pop restaurants in New York, Boston, San Francisco. Every place. You have your Little Italy's and your mom-'n-pop Italian restaurants.

I observed in 1993 – and this was no stroke of genius, by the way – that mom and pop were getting old. Mom and pop were dying, and mom and pop's kids didn't want anything to do with restaurants. So these beloved old institutions that had been around for 30 or 40 years were closing their doors. At the same time, all of these slick Northern Italian-type restaurants with their beveled glass, brass and marble and granite – they were all kind of Epcot iterations of Italian restaurants and just too cool by far – were opening up. I thought, "My God, there is nothing on the horizon that is replacing mom-'n-pop!"

Also, to immigrants that came from southern Italy, abundant food is a symbol of wealth, and family is very important to them. So you say, "Let's just serve a lot of food, and let's just serve it family style."

I built that up to 90 restaurants. After about 25 or 28 restaurants, we took it public, and Planet Hollywood owns it now."

Why was Buca so successful?

Well, I thought that one of the attributes with Buca was that it had to be believable. I didn't want to open up out on restaurant row. And this brownstone building down in the older part of downtown

Minneapolis became available. It was a basement space, and "Buca" means basement or den or cave, or something like that.

It was just a perfect place to test my theory of family-style Italian dining. So we opened it up and, good Lord – and this is not hyperbole – in February in Minnesota, when it's 10 degrees, 15 degrees below zero at times, we would literally have 150 people standing outside. I thought, "Oh shit. Oh dear. Somebody likes this place."

So, I opened a second one. It was really in kind of a dorky market. The first one was in sort of a tony market. There were a lot of condominiums being built, and yuppies were moving in, and all that stuff. But the second one I opened in really kind of a dowdy St. Paul neighborhood in an old supper club that had gone bust. It was a totally different audience. Not as well educated, or anything else.

I'll be damned if we didn't do over $5,000,000 there in our first year. And that was dinner only. With an $18 check average. You can envision the amount of people that we were putting through there.

So then I realized this travels across generations. With two restaurants, it shows that it travels across different incomes, different age groups and different levels of sophistication. I then decided to go to one of the quintessential, white-bread suburbs of Minneapolis called Eden Prairie. The schools are good. The houses are "McMansions." All of that business. I opened up out there, and I'll be damned if the families with the kids didn't just flock there, and we did over $6,000,000 our first year.

Then we decided to take the show on the road and really test it. I thought about Milwaukee, which is about a six-hour drive from here. It's the home of Joe Six-pack. It's not a sophisticated market, but there are a lot of people there. I thought, "Let's try Milwaukee." And I'll be damned if we didn't open in Milwaukee and do $5,000,000 there.

Then I knew I had something that had some legs. My son was with us at the time, and we were talking about expanding. All of the bankers were saying, "You really ought to expand in the Midwest. Go to Des Moines. Go to Duluth. Go to Fargo. Go to Bismarck and Omaha and Kansas City. And that's where you ought to expand."

I thought, "Well, bullshit. I'm not going to travel to cities I don't want to go to. I've done enough traveling in my life. I've got no desire to go to Duluth." So we spread out a map on the conference room table. My son had recently graduated from Stanford business school, and he said, "You know, Dad, Palo Alto is a pretty nice town. I spent a couple of years there." I remember saying, "O.K. That's it. We're going to Palo Alto."

I knew I needed something to startle all of the folks in Silicon Valley because they were getting a lot of restaurants that were all pretty sophisticated and slick. So I decided to design the restaurant so everybody would enter through the kitchen to get to the restaurant. That stood Palo Alto on its ears, and we did $5,000,000 our first year there.

Then we really caught the attention of all of the VCs and bankers and everybody around the country because Palo Alto was such a visible location. So we took in some VC money, and we expanded. A couple of years later we went public.

You're a frequent speaker at conferences and trade shows. What do you typically speak about?

People like to hear how you do it. Where does the idea come from? How do you build around the idea? What about your marketing? In some of our places, we do some very edgy marketing. To the point where it really pisses people off. Which is a good thing because they aren't our customers anyway, but we get a lot of press out of it.

How is your marketing edgy and unique?

It depends on the restaurant. The marketing is a couple of the spokes in that wheel. However you express yourself on the outside has got to describe the promise of what you're going to get on the inside.

Manny's Steakhouse is a good example. We do $17,000,000 a year there. It's all prime beef. I don't know what steakhouses you have there in Charlotte, but it's like The Palm, or Sparks in New York, or any of those.

Manny's symbol from day one has been this really red-eyed, horny bull. Just frothing at the mouth. Just a sexual predator. I mean, that's the look that he has. There's just no doubt that he's kind of a guys-guy kind of a symbol. You can see him on our website (www.mannyssteakhouse.com).

So in our marketing, we always use the bull. When we decided on our meat supplier, he tells us that the American Meat Council had an artist that does marvelous paintings of bulls. The guy is named Frank Murphy.

I called him, and I could tell over the phone that he was a quieter, gentler, older man. I said, "Frank, I need a painting of this bull. And I want him to be the horniest thing you have ever painted in your life. And I want him to be about three feet wide and four feet tall." He says, "Yes, Mr. Roberts, I can do that for you. Why don't I do a pencil sketch, and I'll fax it up to you."

So the next day I get this fax of this bull, and it's really good. I called Frank back and I said, "This looks good. When you paint him I want to make sure that his eyes are red, and that he's really lusting after the cows. And there's one thing I'd like to have you do. I'd like you to make his balls bigger." And this gentle, older man says, "Why, yes Mr. Roberts. I can do that. Why don't I repair the drawing, and I will fax another copy up to you?"

About an hour later, I get this fax, and I call Frank back, and say, "Frank, that's great. You are really moving in the right direction, buddy. But I'd like to have the balls even bigger." He says, "Oh, uh, Mr. Roberts, that would be anatomically incorrect." I said, "Well Frank, let's just do it. I don't give a shit. I'd just like to see them anatomically incorrect."

About an hour later I get another fax, and the balls are damned near hanging on the ground. I call Frank back and I say, "Frank, I've just got one more request." He says, "Oh, Mr. Roberts, what's that going to be?" I say, "I just want you to make 'em shiny."

So his balls are shiny. I mean, you could comb your hair by looking at 'em. But that's the symbol of Manny's. Manny's is a steakhouse, guy's place that women love. It's naughty. You can't believe the number of women that get their pictures taken in front of the bull, tickling his balls. So, you know, it all fits. It's a guys-guy joint.

So that's the way we market Manny's. We always use the bull. And we use him in a number of different ways. Sometimes we only feature his balls in some of our ads. Now, we market Chino Latino in a totally different way.

Tell me about Chino Latino.

Chino Latino was started in 1999. We do about $7,000,000 annually. Open evenings only. It's a small plates restaurant. Flavors exotic to Minnesota.

I came across that idea when my wife and I were in Bangkok, and we just simply noticed that life took place on the street at night, when everybody came out for their social life. And you had all of these little independent food carts selling everything from octopus to who knows what. But they were small plates. The plates were something like $2 or $3.

There was nothing like that anywhere in the U.S. I liked the idea particularly for Minnesota, because you don't want people in Minnesota to bet the farm on a $25 entrée, and then get it and say, "Oh God, I don't like it." There's just way too much Lutheran DNA in Minneapolis, and the people are very conservative. So I thought if I do these small plates, they're spending just $4 or $5 on this little octopus plate that has fish sauce and lime on it. They may or may not like it, but at least they get bragging rights at the water cooler the next morning. "You know what I tried last night? I tried octopus."

You and I might sit down to dinner there, and we might order five small plates for our dinner. So I thought that would be a pretty cool thing to do. But I did worry about it being only Asian, because the incidence of eating Asian food was once every six weeks or so. And I thought, "How could I marry that up with Mexican?" My statistic was that people were eating Mexican every three weeks. So, how do I get those two together?

That's where I came up with the term "Chino Latino," which means "food from around the equator and the hot zone." So that way you could start with the Jamaican jerk chicken, do a Cuban sandwich, do a burrito from Mexico, and a Polynesian drink with an umbrella and a gardenia in it, and then you do a sate from Indonesia and sushi from Japan. You just go right around the world, around the equator.

What kind of marketing do you do there?

As you would expect, Chino draws a younger crowd. Not kids. But the demo for Chino is probably 25 to 40 where Manny's is probably 35 to 60. So I knew that I wanted an edgier kind of message for Chino

Latino when I got around to the marketing of it. I thought that the marketing ought to be a little risky. A little naughty.

Billboards are our main method of communicating for Chino Latino. I ran a billboard that said, "Wok the dog." The hippie crowd went crazy, and we got on TV. We probably got 50...60...$100,000 of publicity on the six o'clock and nine o'clock news, and it had about a three-day cycle, with people standing in front of the billboard, protesting. So we agreed to take it down at the end of the month.

Then I put another one up that said, "Mommy, Mr. Whiskers didn't come home last night." And of course they marched on us again. Well I didn't give a shit. They aren't our customers anyway. But we were getting the publicity. Our sales went up like a hockey stick! And the young people loved it. The young, hipper people – they just loved it.

If you are familiar with Thailand with the resort city of Phuket – they got hit hard by the Tsunami. Well, this was prior to the Tsunami hitting them. Phuket is spelled P-H-U-K-E-T. So I put a billboard up that said, "Aw Phuket. Let's do takeout." I got a call from the principal at Jefferson School, and he said, "Mr. Roberts, I would appreciate it if you would take that billboard down across the street from the school." I said, "Well, why is that?" And he said, "Because of what it says." I said, "Are you referring to the resort city of Phuket, in Thailand?" And he says, "No, you know what I am referring to." I said, "Well tell me." And he says, "Well, here's my problem Mr. Roberts. All the kids are coming home from school, and they are looking up at mom and saying, 'Aw fuckit, let's do takeout,' and I am getting phone calls."

So my point is that kind of marketing fits Chino Latino. It doesn't fit Manny's. It doesn't fit The Good Earth. It doesn't fit Pittsburgh Blue. I doesn't fit Salut. It doesn't fit Muffuletta. So the marketing has to be tailored, and has to be in lockstep with what the concept is.

So it's O.K. to piss people off, as long as you aren't pissing off your core customer base?

That's correct. And you know, people are just wound too tight and that's what pisses me off. They get offended by the least little thing. That just makes me want to tweak 'em more.

Most businesses are trying to please everybody. They aren't clear about who they are.

Yep. It's vanilla.

You seem to have a good eye for looking at things at 30,000 feet. But you also have a good eye for details.

Everything is important. When you sit down at that table, it's important what that tablecloth feels like. The weight of the flatware. The way food is plated. The material in the booth. Is it leather or wood? All of these things contribute to the core of the concept, and it all has to be logical and believable. And yeah, the devil is in the details.

I guess a good example of that would be with Oceanaire. When I created Oceanaire, we were about three or four days from opening and it was about 4:00 in the afternoon. The training class was going to be in at about 4:30, and I went out into the dining room.

The sun was coming through the window, and the highlights were reflecting off of the wine glasses. Every table was set. Everything was in the right place. I mean it was just absolutely beautiful.

And I got scared as hell. I thought, "Oh my God, I've created something that's too fancy, and we'll only do business on Friday and

Saturday night, and on birthdays and anniversaries. And I'll die the rest of the time."

Frankly, it's too late for me to do anything about it. The chairs are in place. You can't take the tablecloths off, because they were plywood table tops with padding on them. So you couldn't do that. I mean, what on earth was I going to do? I mean I had really screwed up on this one.

Then I looked at it for a few minutes and then finally I got an idea. I called Wade, our chef, into the dining room, and I said, "Wade, I want you to order a dozen cases of ketchup." He says, "Well Phil, we don't use ketchup on anything." I said, "I don't give a shit. I want a bottle of ketchup on every single table in this restaurant. And I don't want to stop there. I want packages of those nasty little oyster crackers, wrapped in cellophane. I want those strewn on the center of the table."

The point is that now people can come to the front door of Oceanaire, and they can look in, and does the ketchup bottle actually register with them? Well, maybe, maybe not. But whether they are in a Briani suit or if they are in jeans, they can kind of relate to it. "Yeah, ketchup, this is my kind of place. It's not too fancy."

And it worked. It worked because Oceanaire became a Monday night place for the neighborhood, and it became a Saturday night place where people were spending $100 per person. Oceanaire did $6,500,000 its first year. Dinner only.

Why do so many restaurant partnerships fail?

You can't do a bad partnership with good people. And you can't do a good partnership with bad people.

I was fortunate to have Pete Mihajlov, who I went to college with, and we were buddies. Pete's set of muscles were totally different than mine. Pete is an MBA. He's a business man. He understands debits and credits, and I don't. I brought the creative side to it, and he brought the business side to it.

To be a successful restaurant operation, you better have a cookbook in one hand, and a P&L in the other. So we complement each other in that fashion.

Why do so many restaurants fail in the first few years?

I think it initially looks glamorous, for sure, and the logic sometimes doesn't go any deeper than, "Gee, I sure do like to eat out; it would be fun to own a restaurant." People get into it that way, and they don't realize that some nights you are going to have to mop the dish room floor at three in the morning because the dishwasher quit, or didn't come in. Also, you are working when everybody else is playing. I don't think people think that through.

It's also a very, very capital intensive proposition. Not just the bricks and mortar, but the equipment. If you're going to open a 6,000 square foot restaurant, you better figure about $300 per square foot, all in. So you're going to spend a couple of million bucks, and you're going to have to borrow that, or find angels, or find some way to finance it.

That's risky. And you might just miss. You could miss on several levels. You could miss on location. You could miss on the concept. You could miss on the quality of the food. You could miss on the service. You could just miss on so many levels.

You've got to bring the right food in the back door, and at the right price, and have the right person cooking it, and on the right kind of equipment, and then you better have it delivered efficiently, and the servers better know their stuff, and the dining room better fit the concept, and the table top better fit the concept, and the price better be right. There are so many steps along the way where people could trip up. Any one of those would be bad!

All those spokes in the wagon wheel that you mentioned...

Yeah, all of those spokes in the wagon wheel. It's just got to be seamless. You've got to hit on every single one of them. You could have great food and lousy service, and the restaurant will fail. You could have great service and lousy food. "My steak is overdone. My salad is warm." There are all kinds of nightmare stuff that can go on, so you've got to hit on all of them.

Highlights – A quick recap of Phil's key points...

- ✓ Be great at a few things, not average at a lot of things

- ✓ Check the view from 30,000 feet

- ✓ Edgy marketing gets free PR

- ✓ Be ready to work when everybody else is playing

- ✓ You've got to get every spoke in the wheel right

- ✓ Have a cookbook in one hand, and a P&L in the other

Paranoia, pennies
& paying managers based on profits

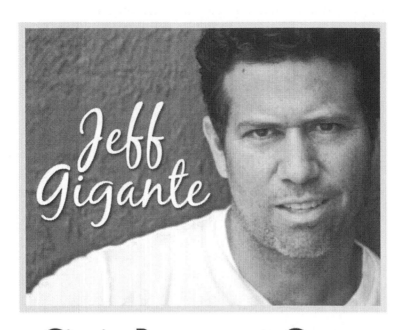

Ciccio Restaurant Group
300+ employees
Tampa Bay and St. Petersburg, FL
Restaurant owner since 1991
www.ciccioandtonys.com

Jeff started his first pizzeria in his final year at Florida State University 20 years ago, and he's been in the restaurant business ever since. This man knows what he's doing. Period. He runs popular, profitable restaurants, and focuses every day on his 300+ staff and the 35,000 people his restaurants (Ciccio's Water, Daily Eats, Lodge, Ciccio's Lodge, Ciccio's California Cuisine, The Lime) serve every week. Want to learn some lessons from a guy who has had every job in the restaurant business, and is now a highly successful owner? Read on...

How did you get started in the restaurant business?

My mother had been a producer for a dinner theatre when I was growing up, and I was bussing tables when I was 10. I have always loved the food industry. I thought it was the coolest thing to be able to do buffets, and serve meals, and drinks, and just entertain. So that was just ingrained in me from being a young guy.

I was going to be graduating from Florida State in 1990 with a theatre degree. I wanted to move to New York to pursue that, but I wanted an income stream so that I wouldn't have to be scrambling to provide that. Meanwhile, my best friend's father had been in the restaurant business for many years. He had the idea of doing a really cool pizzeria.

There was a chain in Tallahassee in the late '80s called Gumby's Pizza. We knew some of the principals there, and they were just killing it, doing $15,000, $17,000 a week, and that was very enticing. So we came up with a model for a place with more of an Italian background. We'd do really great pizza, big sandwiches, salads and pastas.

That's good money for a couple of college guys.

That's what we thought. We ended up borrowing $30,000 from a high school buddy of ours whose family had been very successful. We personally guaranteed the loan, but that meant nothing at that age. [Laughs]

We found a great location … a nine iron up the hill from Florida State. We were right there on the edge, so we knew we could do great delivery service.

We were also right around the corner from a bar called Clydes & Costello's. You'd have to pass our little restaurant in order to get to that bar. So we just thought the location was great. We got it for a very fair rent, and we got a little bit of build-out money from the landlord, and we began work on our pizzeria.

You had no experience. How did the opening go?

[Laughs] My partner's father, who was an Italian immigrant, and a brilliant guy who had done many restaurants and nightclubs, was going to come and show us everything for the first weekend. But something happened and he was called away to Italy.

And here we are, these two college kids, not knowing what kind of pickle we had gotten ourselves into. Everything is ready, everything is in place, except we don't know how to make sauce. We don't know how to make the dough. And pizza is a science. It's an Old World craft of baking, and it doesn't leave a lot of room for error.

After several hours of trying to figure it out on our own with books, we realized we were up the river without a paddle. So we arranged to make a phone call with my partner's dad. And we literally had a four-hour phone call, and it ended up costing at least $400.

We kept running back and forth from the phone at the front of the store to the back where the kitchen and the ovens were. We had this long hallway, and we kept running back and forth, back and forth, kneading the dough, watching the dough rise, and everything he told us to do. But it was very worth it, because we ended up perfecting the dough and the sauce and the whole process.

The next night was the town Christmas lighting night. We were able to sell pizzas out in front of the restaurant, because we weren't completely ready inside. And everyone went nuts for the pizza. They said it was the best pizza they had ever tasted. So we were just thrilled. We opened inside the next day, and we had a very successful first year.

Did you end up living up to that personal guarantee?

Yes. We had borrowed the $30,000 from our friend, and we also gifted him 5% equity in the business, which ended up being worth nothing. It was a huge learning experience for us all.

We were making regular payments as well as we could. And about a year after we opened, I moved to New York to follow my dream of becoming an actor. My partner took on another partner or two. And it didn't go the way that it was going when I was there. They ended up giving away the business for pennies on the dollar.

Luckily our investor was good enough to split that $30,000 between my partner and I, and I successfully paid him back over the next two-and-a-half years.

What was the biggest lesson you learned from that experience?

First, don't go into business with your best friends. I think successful business relationships come from being able to leave emotion out of it. But when you have lifetime experiences with a best friend, you get very personally, emotionally involved, and then you get your feelings hurt. That on top of business mindset and outlook differences can lend itself to a whole lot of problems. How do you separate business and personal relationships? And if you have to part ways, how does that not affect the friendship?

The second lesson was that you've got to understand some simple accounting and business practices. Whether they are right or wrong, you've got to commit to some way of doing the back end. For example: Monies come in for sales. Well, what buckets do they go into? We have to have a bucket for sales tax. We have to have a bucket for rent. We have to have a bucket for salaries.

Also, how do you pay yourself? Are you just going to take what you need? Are you just going to say, "O.K., everybody gets $300 per week until we get our feet underneath us?" which is probably the way we should have done it. But we weren't doing that. We would all work 60, 70 hours, and then on Saturday night when we slowed down, we'd want to go to the bars and blow off steam. We'd each take $100 out of the drawer. Some people got very comfortable with that notion, and others weren't. So that creates problems.

I was focused on managing the staff, and scheduling, and training, and portion control, and all of that stuff. I had a partner who fantasized about having a financial background, and he wanted to take care of the books. And that was a huge, huge problem.

What happened in New York?

I needed an income, so I got a job in New York at a place called Coastal, which was a very famous fish restaurant in the late '80s through the mid '90s. It was owned by the Lanza family, who owned several other restaurants.

Within a month I was on the floor, and just hopping around to their different restaurants. I was like the utility guy. If I were scheduled for four nights, the other four nights I'd get dressed for work and show up at one of the restaurants and just beg servers to go. "Listen, you've got something you could do with your girlfriend." Or, "Your wife is in a Broadway show." Or whatever. I'd say, "Go have fun. Let me work here." And nine times out of 10, somebody would be happy to have the shift off when you had 10 to 15 servers. Somebody's always not wanting to be there.

Sounds like you were determined to be successful.

Yes. I was pretty much working seven nights a week. Saving money and paying down my debt from the pizzeria. And I was very impressed with how these guys ran a business. Jimmy, who is my partner now, was an accountant by trade. He was very savvy on the back end of a restaurant. He was so organized.

I became a manager for them next, and I really ingrained myself in the back office so I could right the wrongs that had happened down in Tallahassee and learn the back end.

Did you keep acting as well?

Yes, but by this time, my acting career was going up and down. I booked a four-month contract on a soap opera called "Loving", and I finally felt like I had made my break. It was good money. It starred Kelly Ripa and Randy Manson. But three weeks after I signed that contract, they canceled the show.

Meanwhile, my restaurant career was solid. I was really becoming an asset, and people were looking up to me. And I really felt at home. So when they cancelled the soap opera, I kind of took that as a sign from the gods.

So you set your sights on the restaurant business?

Yes. I kept at it, and was saving every penny I could. Outside of restaurants, I was selling fitness equipment, and I was a personal trainer. I was doing anything I could so that I could have some sort of bank account so I could get my own place.

I knew that wasn't going to be in New York City. I was from St. Petersburg, FL, and Tampa Bay was a hustling and bustling little town just outside of St. Pete, so my thought process was to go back there.

After about four or five years of doing this grind, I saved about $40,000. And I got confirmation from family and friends down in Florida, that if I did the same Italian concept down in Tampa, it would kill.

I should add that I grew up in a meager environment. We didn't have much money. My father passed away when I was very young, so I had a single mom. We discount shopped, and didn't eat out a lot. And although my mom was a very hard worker and a good earner, there weren't a lot of dollars to stretch. So my goal when I was young was to make $100,000 per year. That was a big goal, and if I could ever get there, I would be rich.

So you were focused on making $100,000 per year, and that helped drive you?

Yes, that was the goal that was still driving me. Maybe if I could get down to Florida, and we could do some good numbers, then I could reach that goal. So I talked to my friends' families, and got some commitments.

Finally, after four or five years, I go to Jim, and I tell him, "I want to move back to Florida and do this concept. I can get investors, and I need you to invest. I'd like you to go to Florida for three or four months, and help me get this place open."

He agreed. This was in early '96. We found a location we liked, negotiated a lease, and got busy. He was commuting down a few times per month, and when he wasn't there, I was calling him every day. And of course for me, this was the best thing in my life. I was going to be an owner of a business.

What kind of research did you do to find your location?

The research I did was from trusted family and friends. When we were making trips down here to look for locations, I would get them to put us in a car and drive us around and show us the different areas of town.

Ybor City [in Tampa], for example. That area was attractive for some reasons. But then they would tell us that it was a weekend place, and it was young, and there's not a lot of money down there, and on the weekdays it's kind of dead. Meanwhile, we wanted to be a neighborhood place, so we looked at different areas. We were looking at Tampa through the eyes of these people that had made their lives here. Successful doctors, attorneys and business people.

They knew which areas were hot, or dead, or up-and-coming. They'd drive us to the areas that we liked, and then they'd drive us all around the area, and show us the different homes, and that type of thing. And I think that type of research is invaluable.

Not to mention that we would also go out and eat lunch and dinner two or three days in a row in all of these areas that we were looking at, to just kind of get a feel for what kinds of people were eating in those places, and how busy they were at different times.

So that's really all of the research that we did. Being on the streets, and eating in the restaurants, and talking to everybody that would listen. Going in to the busy places and finding out who the manager was, and talking to them.

Lots of restaurants fail. What separates the ones that succeed from the ones that fail?

I think it's the scrutiny that you use. We've always had an air of paranoia. When we're busy, we want to be busier. When we're not so busy, then we're really concerned, and we start introspectively looking at everything.

I'm a perfectionist, so that means that I'm not ever fully pleased with how things are going. I'm cautiously optimistic when things are good, but I always know that at any given time, things could fall flat.

You also have to pay close attention to your cost controls. When I was a 15-year-old busboy working for Chili's, I'll never forget what the manager told me. He said, "Son, this is a business of pennies. You watch the pennies, and the dollars will take care of themselves." And I would catch him on more than one occasion out back, sifting through garbage, finding all of the packets of ketchup and salt and pepper and the plastic silverware that was still in its wrapper. He'd say, "This affects my bottom line. We pay hard pennies for this, and people throw them away. And that's unacceptable."

A "penny business," huh?

You bet. I've always been cost crunching, and paranoid about the money, because I want to protect my income fiercely, and voraciously. So this is what I've done, and it's really helped.

I'm not even saying that we're the most successful restaurateurs. I'm sure that people profit a lot better than we do. But we've been consistently earning and profiting better than nine out of 10 restaurants around us.

Do you hire managers from the outside or promote from within?

I can't remember a manager or assistant manager that hasn't started at a lower position in our restaurant. We really believe in growing people. It takes them time to get in, work under our tutelage, and then adapt the mindset that we try to live by.

It's hard to hire somebody from the outside, with all of their thoughts and expectations and philosophies, and have them come in and try to meld with what we're doing. It's much better to have servers that grow to head servers, and say, "You know what? I love what you guys do. It would be a dream for me to have a piece of this."

I understand you also have general managing partners who buy into the business.

We've financed a lot of our partners that ended up becoming general managing partners of our business after they've been managers for a couple of years, and they want a piece of it.

For me, it's very important that people are willing to put skin in the game, because then they're truly vested like we are. They live and die by the success of the business. It's easy for a GM who's making $60,000 a year to become indifferent to the bottom line. For example, if he sees a server throw out a plastic tray that costs me 89 cents, and he doesn't dive in there to get it and then grab the server and say, "Listen, this is not garbage." When somebody's got their salary and they're comfortable, it's hard for them to have those types of eyes.

But when they know that they've borrowed money from their mother, and stuck it into this restaurant, and she's calling and saying, "How is it doing son? Are you doing O.K.? Are you making money?

You made a $2,200 bonus at the end of this month? That's phenomenal!" That's a different aspect altogether. That's the people we're looking for. Because this is my passion. This is what I do to take care of my family.

I'm honestly and truly thinking of all of our 300 plus employees, as well as the 35,000 people we feed every month. Those people are in the foremost of my mind, because those are the people that create the life that I'm able to lead and give to my family. I'm very appreciative of it, and very protective of it.

Is it common for restaurants to be structured that way?

I have friends that own restaurants, but I don't really see other people doing that. It is a risk. You're sharing profits, and some people just like to have employees.

We've never looked at it that way. In essence, part of it is kind of like the way that Outback started and grew to such a large number. They had a general managing partner deal. We adapted some of that to our way of doing things, and not making the requirements be that they're liquid for so much money.

We're selfishly looking for people that are going to "out-care" us in what we're doing. It's hard to find those people. But we've found some great partners that have really risen through the ranks. I don't think our structure is the norm, but I think it should be.

How do you keep your customers coming back again and again?

That's a very important question. We do a myriad of different things. First of all, we have the mindset that if the customer is not pleased for any reason, you've got to do something for that table. Even if they've eaten the whole meal, and they say, "You know what guys? We eat here all of the time, and you guys are great. But this meal was a little off." They've eaten the whole meal, so a lot of people will say, "O.K., we'll try to do better for you next time." Not us. We'll buy that meal. We'll deduct that from their bill, and thank them for letting us know.

The customers are usually pretty "on" about our food. When we check with the chef, a lot of times we'll come back out and say, "You know what? That was the bottom end of that sauce run. And it shouldn't have been served. You're totally right. Thanks for letting us know that." And this way you give that customer a feeling of participation in what we're doing.

Jim and I and our managers have this mindset: If the customer is unhappy, you've got to do something to please them in the immediate moment in order for them to know that you care and that you're trying to make it right.

What else keeps 'em coming back?

We also do specials bi-monthly. Every other week at every restaurant. And every 18 to 30 months, we change something at every restaurant. Whether it be a painting change, or striping the parking lot, or new furniture, or barstools. A TV here or there. Landscaping. We always do something to freshen things up. And that all falls back to that same feeling of being paranoid.

If we know of a new restaurant that's opening, we try to do something before they open. We want people to say, "Wow, these Ciccio guys are always doing something. We're putting awnings on a building. We're taking awnings off. We're putting drapes on a building. It's constantly an ebb and flow of showing that we're putting money back into the building.

When Jim and I travel we look for new ideas for food. He found this bowl on a trip that had chopped lettuce, and warm rice, and chicken, and cucumbers, etc. So we played around with that idea, and created it on our menu.

Most people are afraid to change the menu that has made them successful, but I think of a restaurant as a living, breathing, organism. And if you're not constantly evolving, you're going to be dead in the water. There are constantly going to be new places opening, and new experiences. And people are going to say, "Well, why would we go back there? They have 10 menu items." That's not the case. We try to keep things flowing.

Which concept has the most potential for growth?

Daily Eats is our diner, and I really believe it's the future growth of our company. It's very easily packageable. If you ate there, you'd understand instantly. It's a place that you could put in any beach town, mall, hotel lobby, city center or any airport. And people are going to say, "There's something here for everyone. They've got a value menu. This is a good deal for the money."

It's got incredible margins, and it has a limited menu. If you go online and look at the Ciccio's Water menu, you'll say, "How in the 'F' do these guys do this menu?" That menu is good. It's evolved and grown over the years. But that's not an easily replicable menu. You can't just put a new restaurant guy and a kitchen guy into that menu and think that they're going to have success in every category. Sushi, pizza, pastas, salads, fish, steaks, veal. You just can't do it. You would never dream to do that to somebody.

The Daily Eats concept is eggs, burgers, shredders, and all of these things that we've created. I'm confident that I could go in the kitchen

– and I haven't cooked in 10 years – and pretty much make anything on that menu, and have it be 80% as good as how my chef makes it.

That's big. That's huge. You want something that's manageable, that's not a huge footprint. It's about 2,800 square feet. So when you're as busy as you can be, you've got 120 guests. It's very doable for expansion. Right now, we do anywhere from $1,300,000 to $1,700,000 a year, in a little place like this – on more than 20% profit margins. Those are good numbers.

You and Jim stay very involved, and paranoia helps drive your success. Will you be able to scale that to remote locations?

That's a great point. That's where the leap of faith with what we've done through the years and being able to put the controls in place with the people that we choose will come in. And we'll see how it goes. You can't be everywhere at once. You've got people that grow restaurant chains to 1,000 units. No one can be in 1,000 units.

So I think if we're going to do what I'm planning on doing, we've got to get really über strong on our controls, and the back-end books, and the menu books, and our ideology. We have all of that. It's just got to be fine tuned.

We'll grow the Daily Eats chain within our area where we can touch it daily. And then we'll raise up from our current employee base some people that really want to grow these concepts, and have the background to do so. And just take it one step at a time.

Highlights – A quick recap of Jeff's key points...

✓ Don't be partners with your best friends

✓ A little paranoia is good

✓ It's a business of pennies

✓ Enable general managing partners to put skin in the game for a piece of the business

✓ You better evolve or you'll die

✓ Keep it simple if you want to expand

Soul, sexiness
& competing for staff instead of
customers

Tria Restaurant
Biba Wine Bar
50+ employees
Philadelphia, PA
Restaurant owner since 2004
www.triacafe.com
www.bibawinebar.com

Jon Myerow didn't come from money. He's a guy who took on equity and debt to start his first Tria location in 2004, and he's worked very hard every year since to build popular, profitable restaurants. He has learned to mix in style and creativity with hard work and savvy business decisions. Along the way, he has created Philadelphia's most popular wine, cheese and beer cafés, featuring artisanal products made by passionate people. Both Tria and Biba are simple concepts, executed extremely well. Jon shares great advice for any restaurant owner or aspiring owner…

How did you get started in the restaurant business?

I have a degree in Russian language, but I thought it would be fun to be in the restaurant business. [Laughs] When I graduated college, I became a buss person in a restaurant of which I was a customer.

I wasn't a very good buss person, and the owners didn't think I would last in the business at all. But I worked for them for four years. I became a GM, and opened up a restaurant for them. I went and got an MBA, and then decided to become partners with them in a restaurant in Philadelphia in 1992. That restaurant was open until 2000, but toward the end I was doing some consulting and other things.

In 2000 I took a job as director of operations for Neil Stein, who was a well known Philadelphia restaurant operator. He had five restaurants, but he ended up in jail a few years later for all sorts of tax fraud. It wasn't a very tightly run company, but I learned a lot about concepts and other things like how the size of a space can affect you in a restaurant, and how design can affect people's reactions, and so forth.

Toward the end, the company was sort of unraveling, and I knew I had to get out. The concept for Tria literally came to me when I was having dinner at a friend's house. Their dinner consisted of Belgian ale, cheese, fruit and bread. To me, there was actually a business concept in there.

The idea I had of putting wine, cheese and beer together was a natural for me, because I love both wine and beer, but – at least in Philadelphia – they've been very segregated. One is elite and one is blue collar. You'd find good glasses of wine in the bars of fine-dining restaurants, and then other restaurants would have pretty standard, industrial wine. Philadelphia is a pretty amazing beer city, but most of the beer establishments are pretty frat party-like.

I thought they should be in the same place – somewhere you could wear your blue jeans, but also feel comfortable taking a date. The idea was to put them in the same room, and force them to get along. And while cheese and wine is obviously a long time culinary marriage, our assertion is that beer and cheese is even a better combination. They go really well together. I don't think it had been done before, but it was very natural to me.

What was your timeline for going from one location, to two, to three?

We started the first Tria in 2004, and then we opened the second one in 2007. In 2006 we opened the Tria Fermentation School, because most of what we sell is not mainstream. It's not industrial. It's all small production. People come into a place like Tria, and the whole menu is alien to them.

Education has always been a part of the concept, in a friendly way. We built a classroom in an office building, which has 24 seats. We've been doing classes for four years now, with a lot of world famous wine makers and brewers, cheese makers, importers. It's an amazing cast of people that have come in here to do classes on what they do and sell.

And then this year (2010) we just launched Biba wine bar, which is a more streamlined version of Tria, with all communal seating. It's a very European concept. It's a place to go and grab a few glasses of wine with your friends and have a snack, and maybe meet other people. The communal seating aspect is kind of like a wine and cheese party that never stops. People are sort of mingling and hanging out and drinking wine, or beer, and just having a good time.

So it's sort of institutionalizing a wine and cheese party as a business concept. It's only been open 10 days or so, but the initial response has been really positive.

How important was it to put together a solid business plan?

It was critical because we had to raise money. To be frank, a lot of restaurant owners are wealthy people who are doing it for fun. I'm not in that category. I don't come from money. This is my livelihood, so our restaurants have been roughly half debt, half equity … with a lot of begging.

The equity initially came from friends, but now it's coming from customers, and outsiders that aren't familiar with me. As for the debt, the banks really wouldn't touch this. But we've managed to get debt financing from a local, quasi-government, quasi-private organization that exists to fund businesses that create jobs in the city of Philadelphia. They do it with a lot of restrictions, but low interest rates. These people demand very well-developed plans, and they look at every cent you spend.

With Biba, I'm looking back at the business plan, at the financials, to see how it's tracking versus what I projected. You know, you don't do a business plan just for the outside world. You do it for yourself. You have to have some discipline. And it's like, "Wait, I projected that there'd be two people in the kitchen, and there's three. And it's a little bit slow tonight, so it's completely throwing our labor budget out of line, so we have to make some adjustments."

You don't really have a boss, or somebody to report to. But if you have a business plan to report to, it does give you the discipline you need.

What advice do you have for people considering co-owning with a partner?

Well, it really is like getting married. Having complementary strengths is great, but many partnerships don't work out. My advice would be not to become partners with someone unless you have already worked with them. My partner Michael was an employee for several years before we felt comfortable making him a partner.

I actually started out with a potential partner, who was a wine person, and that ended up in litigation before we even opened. So I know all too well what can happen.

I think the other thing to do is to make sure your lawyers have a plan when things go sour. If things are not able to be reconciled, there should be an exit strategy in place before you need it. If things go south, the person to be is the one who is going to go and sell his shares under a certain formula. Otherwise everybody's investment will probably get destroyed.

What about finding the right investors, and making sure their expectations are aligned with yours?

Yeah, if you have a red flag about an investor before they sign on the dotted line, it's probably best to not go through with it. But I think the important thing is to make sure legally that everything is clear. That you are upfront with everything.

I tell every potential investor that there is a reasonable chance that they're going to lose their entire investment. So if that would affect their life or their lifestyle, then it's not the investment for them.

The other thing is to communicate with them. Let them know the positives and the negatives, so they don't feel like, "Hey, what's this guy doing with my money?"

I think as long as people think you're being honest, and acting in good faith to make money for them and for the company, then you should be O.K. But if you ignore people, then they're going to start to think the worst if they're not seeing returns as quickly as they might want.

Were there times early on when you thought to yourself, "What am I doing? What have I gotten myself into?"

Well, yeah, I did. I worked without a salary for two years. I had influential business people tell me my idea was stupid, and that nobody would go. Banks laughed at me. It's a very lonely road.

The funny thing is, in Pennsylvania there's no such thing as a beer and wine license. So pretty much every restaurant that has alcohol has distilled spirits, as well as wine and beer, because you can. Other states have beer and wine licenses. The day we opened, my lawyer partner said, "What the hell are we doing opening up a bar in Rittenhouse Square – which is a very influential part of the city – with no martinis?" The first customer to ever walk in said, "Where's the martini?" and then walked out because we didn't have one. I just wanted to shoot myself. [Laughs]

It took time, because there were no other wine bars like this in Philadelphia. There were plenty of times where I was thinking, "What am I doing?" In spite of that, I always believed in the concept.

It was a place that I would want to go. I didn't believe that other people wouldn't want to go there as well, because I don't think my tastes are that insane.

The first one was slow to take off, but the sales in 2009 were nearly double what they were our first full year (2005). Sales have gone up at both locations every single year, and we've never done any media advertising since we started. It's all been through word-of-mouth and internally generated marketing.

You have to believe in what you're doing, and you have to stay true to it. The Phillies have been doing really well every year, and part of our concept is that we don't have TVs. It's a place to go and talk to your friends. It's pretty basic. Well, the last three years during the baseball playoffs, man, I wish I had a big TV. Because during the playoffs, the Phillies games start, and the place empties out. But you can't sell yourself. You have to keep true to your concept. Or else, no one's going to know what you stand for.

You touched on something that seems so important, but lots of people miss: Know who you are, and have a clear, simple concept.

We have a very focused concept. The fact is, Tria is not for everybody. Not everyone drinks wine. Our menu is pretty Euro-centric. Not much of it is mainstream, so a lot of people wouldn't want to go there.

But that's the thing. Now you're going to appeal to people who will become stark-raving fans. The interesting thing is, Tria is *superficially* a simple concept. But it's not that simple to run. That was the reason we did Biba, because it is easier than Tria to run. Making something simple is actually quite complicated. What a paradox! We have very small menus, but an extraordinary amount of time goes into choosing the selections and into educating the staff on them.

Look at beer. There are 1,500 registered brands, and six distributors. There are websites that post what's hot and what's not. So even though I put a lot of time into the beer list, it's relatively simple.

But with wine, there's no transparency. There are dozens and dozens of importers, and hundreds of thousands of little wineries. It takes Michael a lot of work and dealing with a lot of people to choose the wines. Most places won't do that. We have clout because we have three locations now, and we can get some stuff that other people can't get. So we have a simple concept, but we also have been trying to build a competitive advantage that other people can't copy. You're not going to be able to compare wine lists, to a certain extent.

Restaurants have a notoriously low barrier to entry. Anyone can open up a restaurant. So what we've tried to do is have a very focused concept, with an emphasis on service and on educating our guests, which makes it harder to copy.

How did things change for you when you opened your second location?

Well, opening another location was always the plan. We believe in what we do, and we think people should be drinking good wine on every corner in the city, not just on one corner. We sell products that we are crazy about, and they are made by people we know, in many cases. And these are artists. They're not multi-national companies.

I put a lot of work – more than most people I think – into building an infrastructure first. And frankly, it's completely damaged our profitability, because we built an infrastructure for multiple units before we had multiple units.

For example, we have food cost software that we've probably spent $28,000 on so far. Usually the type of organization that would buy that would be a larger chain, or a large resort or casino or something. But we bought it. We have enterprise reporting from our POS system. We can get information immediately. We have a full-time person who focuses on training and hiring and all of that stuff. The level of detail in all of the systems is just a lot more involved than most mom-'n-pop restaurants. And with Biba, I've taken it to an even higher level of organizational systems.

Where do you go from there?

You get it to where you want to grow bigger, but have a company that has some soul to it. You know, where it's not like "McWinebar." That's what we're trying to do. It's frustrating. But it's challenging, and I like challenges.

How do you grow but maintain your company's "soul"?

Your culture and passion can do the work for you. If everyone has the same passion for being here — for the products, for giving great service — half of our job is done. When we grow, nothing suffers.

Is it challenging to find people for your team that share the passion that you have?

Yeah, it is. There are a lot of people with the passion for the product. Luckily, we sell something that a lot of people love. But the secret is to find somebody who has the passion for it, and also has the ability to be a good restaurant employee.

We've hired some people with the passion, but they just weren't very good on the floor. Some people just can't be good servers. I'm one of them, so I feel their pain. But I think we've done a good job with that. We're very selective. If we put an ad on Craigslist, we'll get 100 or 200 responses, and there might be three or four people that we consider seriously.

I like to say, "It's harder to get into Tria than it is to get into Harvard!" [Laughs] Our acceptance rate is lower. And our employees know that. I think the people that work here know that they put up with a lot, but they get a lot back. We try to give much better tangible benefits to our staff than other restaurants because we expect a lot.

We have quizzes every single week, and training every single week for every single front-of-house staff member. If you don't want to learn a lot in your free time about wine, beer and cheese, you're going to get fired. It's that simple.

To me the biggest competition is not for customers. It's for staff. If you compete in the labor market and get the best staff, the customers will follow.

How do you figure out during the interview process which people can actually do the job?

We have a lot of steps. We put an ad that says, "Send a cover letter and a resume. And if you don't send a cover letter indicating why you would be a good fit here, we will definitely not respond to you." And 30% of the people can't follow that simple instruction. So that weeds out 30%.

The cover letter has to show some definite interest in the products, and show a background that can be compatible. They don't have to have college degrees, but they usually do. Or they show a huge interest in the arts or something. There's a certain profile that usually fits. But these are interested people that have shown a passion for something, and also show passion for wine. Then there are two interviews: one with me, one with Michael. They also have to take a written test during the application process.

If all of that goes well, they come back for on-the-job experience at one of the restaurants. They get to hang out with the manager and the staff, and those people give feedback on what it's like to work with the applicant. So it's a pretty expensive and lengthy process to hire someone. A lot of people say, "Well they're just going to quit in a year anyhow, so why do you care?"

Well, these people control the restaurant. They are the front line. If they last a year, that's great. If they last five years – which we've had – that's even better. But we take this incredibly seriously. And even then, we've made some mistakes. We've hired maybe 15 new people on the floor in the last three months, and two thirds, maybe three quarters worked out. Two or three people didn't work out. A few people, I'm on the fence about. So despite our best efforts, it's not always going to work.

We've gotten better at cutting our losses earlier, because it's really not doing them a favor to keep them there, when really none of us see any chance of them succeeding in this environment. I think we used to be a lot slower to part ways with people that we know in our hearts, and intellectually, aren't going to work out.

Why is the design of your restaurant so important?

It's very important. For Biba, I made it very clear what I wanted the design to do, and how I wanted it to make you feel. People walk in, and they want to be there.

It costs a lot of money to hire an architect at the level that can accomplish that. And a lot of the finishes are very expensive. With the design, once you do it you don't have to put any more effort into it, except to keep it clean and maintained.

Everything in this place is contextual. I think I learned that working for Neil Stein. He used to own a restaurant called Striped Bass, which was one of the top five seafood restaurants in the country. The room was just magnificent. The fish entrees were $35 or $40 apiece. Sometimes I would eat them in my fluorescent-lit office, and it wouldn't be the same. There's no way you can say it tastes the same while sitting in an office, versus in this magnificent room.

So we have a room that makes people feel … sexier. And just warmer. That adds value to the experience, and it will make people want to come back.

Do you get inspiration for design outside of your industry?

Yes. So for instance, take Apple. The cleanness of the design is incredible. It's inspirational. I like that clean, minimal aesthetic, and that's what we always look for.

I look at retail spaces and other restaurants from a space standpoint. There's a wine store in Sonoma, CA that I go to every time I am there. There is a little bar in the back, with maybe six seats. People just walk in, and hang out, and drink there, and talk. That's always been a major influence on me. I just like the feeling of the place, and I've always tried to achieve that.

Why did you decide to launch the Tria Fermentation School?

Well, I hate to use the "B" word, but it does promote our brand as the place where you learn about these things. But honestly, the biggest benefit has been with the relationships with the instructors, because there's nothing else quite like it. When people teach a class here, they feel an attachment to Tria, and they want their products here.

Who teaches?

For brewers we've had everything from Lambic brewers in Belgium to rock star American brewers, like Sam Calagione from Dogfish Head. The winemakers wouldn't be household words. Every wine growing country – Spain, France, Australia – has important winemakers. We've had the owner of Ravenswood in California do two classes here. That's a hugely important American winery. We've had most of the major beer importers do classes. We've had a lot of wine importers. And Michael teaches a lot of the classes too, so we do a lot of in-house stuff like "Wine 101" and so forth.

Do the people who come to your classes become frequent customers?

Oh yeah. These are the advocates who go around and sing our praises. The classes keep them very happy. And it's important on both levels.

The school doesn't really make money, but it's an important part of our identity. It's sort of our mascot. It's always going to be with us I think.

So you've done no traditional advertising?

None. We only do internal marketing. We have an email list of 18,000 people. We send emails usually once a week, and we do certain in-house promotions.

For example, every Sunday we feature a wine, beer and cheese at close to half price. We try to focus on stuff that people wouldn't naturally gravitate to. We encourage them to try new things with a low financial risk. If you want to get people out of chardonnay and pale ale and cheddar, you have to bribe them a little bit.

Now Sundays are one of our busiest days of the week, when originally it was one of our slowest days of the week. We don't make as much of a profit on it, but we're educating our customers to new things, and they're going to be a better consumer. They're going to wonder why other places don't have things like these products.

So it's a way of getting people to want more of what we have. That's been going on for five years now. It's a promotion, but it's all internal. There are so many externally-based promotions available now, on the Internet and so forth, but I just think it's more fun to do it ourselves, and to control it and to keep it tasteful.

What does the future hold?

Trying to get a day off. [Laughs] Once I do that, I think Biba will be more easily replicated than Tria. Once we get this running smoothly, we'll probably look for another location that would be appropriate for Biba, and we'll take it from there.

Highlights – A quick recap of Jon's key points...

- ✓ **A good business plan helps you stay disciplined**

- ✓ **Believe in what you're doing, and stay true to it**

- ✓ **It's complicated to make something simple**

- ✓ **Don't be easy to copy**

- ✓ **Compete for staff, not customers**

- ✓ **Sex appeal adds value to the customer experience**

-

Small towns, pearls
&why most startup books are wrong

Socorro Springs Restaurant & Brewery
Eddyline Restaurant & Brewery
90+ employees
Socorro, NM and Buena Vista, CO
Restaurant owner since 1999
www.socorrosprings.com
www.eddylinepub.com

Mic and Molley Heynekamp started Socorro Springs Restaurant & Brewery in 1999. After four and a half years of planning, they took their original $1,000,000 business plan down to $100,000. And they wound up starting with only $70,000. Ten years later they opened Eddyline Restaurant & Brewery. Both restaurants have been very successful, and Mic and Molley plan to open a third in May 2011. How could you not want to learn from a guy that started with 7% of what he initially thought it would take to get started, and made it work – extremely well? Mic runs lean and highly profitable restaurants, and he had quite a few pearls of wisdom to share...

How did you get involved with owning restaurants?

For me, it was kind of an accident. For Molley, it was her goal for a long time. That's why she went to college and got an accounting degree. I was home brewing beer just as a hobby while I was getting my geology degrees. My path was to be a geologist, mainly for the travel and outdoor opportunities.

So five or six of us were climbing the San Juan Mountains in southwestern Colorado and we started wondering how we could live in a cool little mountain town? Our degrees weren't going to do it for us for sure. After we got down from the mountains, we went to this little brewpub called Carver's Brewery & Bakery, and met with the brew master. And it just kind of came to me: "Molley wants to own a restaurant. I love home brewing. Let's do the two together and see what we can make of it."

The next year she had to write a business plan for her senior class. We visited a lot of brewpubs around the southwest, and got a lot of ideas, and got a bunch of information and did a whole business plan on it. Once we started looking at it – the projections and stuff – we realized that not only would this be our ticket to living in a small town, but we could actually make a good living at it. The whole thing just really appealed to us and intrigued us. You don't have a boss. You can do your own deal. You can have a lot of creativity and flexibility. So what better thing could there be?

What steps did you take next?

At the end of the year (1995), she graduated, and we started talking to people. We went to Pagosa Springs, CO, and we started talking to realtors and talking to bankers.

We got totally laughed out of the first banker's office. He thought we were a bunch of jokers. So that was a bit of a wake-up call. In our original business plan, we estimated that we needed $1,000,000 for everything. We were planning for brand new, top-of-the-line equipment, and so on. So he kind of laughed at us, and told us, "You've got to go back and get your costs way down. And you need to have your own money coming into this thing." He pretty much told us it was impossible.

I started grad school around the same time, and we just kept trying. We looked at several little towns, and we thought we had really trimmed down our business plan. We got it down to about $700,000, so we went to a banker and told him how we had really made our plan into a lean business plan. He pretty much laughed us out the door.

You kept at it though...

You bet. We were living in Socorro Springs, NM, and one of our friends knew the owner of an old historic building. A gentleman named Chuck. We showed Chuck our plan and told him what we wanted to do, and he was real interested. But at the same time, he told us, "You're nuts for putting that much money out there with no experience. You'll never make it work. You've got to find a way to get it down."

Then we went to the Great American Beer festival, and we stopped in at a place called Il Vacino, which is now Amica's Restaurant and Brewery, in Salida, CO. There was a great person there named Tom Hennessy, and he had put out this video called "How to Start Your Own Micro-Brewery for Less than $20,000." In it he talked about how to use old dairy equipment, and how to improvise. You don't have to buy everything new and turnkey.

He had this tiny little kitchen. One four-burner stove and a wood-fired pizza oven. He told us the wood-fired pizza oven was awesome. It was relatively inexpensive, real efficient, you could cook a pizza in it in about three minutes, and it's unique. Meanwhile pizzas have a really low cost of goods, and you only need one prep table, and you can get by with pretty much nothing in terms of the kitchen.

On the way back we looked at a bunch of other breweries that were really thriving with really efficient, small setups, and not a lot of overhead. We came back home and Molley went to work crunching numbers, and our $500,000 to $700,000 startup shrank down to about $100,000.

We went back to Chuck and said, "We've learned a bunch of things, and we think we need less than $100,000 to get started. We've already been buying some of the equipment we'll need." He looked up with an excited look, and said, "OK. Let's at least try it."

So our discussions started, and about a year later we opened. It was about four and a half years from the time we said we were going to own a restaurant until the day we opened. That's how we got into this business. We just kept pushing and pushing.

Your initial business plan was $1,000,000 and you got it down to $100,000?

Correct. Since then, we always find ways to save money. For example, that building was leased, and we were in there the first six years. At the end of our lease we had to buy a building, or build one. We found a great location and decided to build one.

We went into it with architects, and they told us it was going to be about $3,000,000. We said there was no way we could do that, and we had to get that price down.

So we went back to the same lessons we learned to help us get started. When you look at all of the startup books, they say "Make sure you are well funded, and you don't skimp on equipment. Only use the best of the best." They are wrong. That strategy puts you much closer to failure, because if you have a bad month or so, that's it. You have so much money at risk. Whereas if you can do it really lean, you are way better off.

So the architects kept saying, "You are talking about 7,000 square feet, and you can't do it for under $400 per square foot." So that's $2,800,000 without any equipment. So we kept going back and forth with them.

Finally Molley and I thought, "We have a buildable set of plans. Let's walk away from them and tell them we don't want to do business with them anymore. Because these guys don't get it." We took those plans to different builders and said, "Here are the plans. You're welcome to make changes. We want you to bid it at the cheapest you can, and just give us a list of the changes that you would require to get it to that price." We said we wanted it to be around $500,000.

They all looked at us like we were totally crazy, except one builder who told us he could do it for $600,000. We said, "All right. Let's do it!" Half way through the project, we had to fire him, but I had construction experience from high school, so I took it over and finished it out myself. We still got opened on time, and under budget, and it's still cranking away today.

So with a debt load of about a quarter of what it was going to be originally, that means we have that much more leftover so we can be that much more competitive than any other place.

How did you get that original $100,000 you needed when you first got started?

Well, the banks wouldn't have anything to do with us, so we'd go around to restaurants that had gone out of business, and we'd buy what we could. We were just using credit cards, and I had just finished up grad school, so I maxed out all of my student loans to the extent I could.

There was also a lot of stuff we could get for free. For example, we went to a dairy, and the man had a tank sitting out. I asked him how much he'd sell it for, and it was $50! So we ended up buying a lot of stuff that way. Once we'd done all of that, we realized we needed about $30,000 more to finish the building out. We ended up getting the landlord to carry that in a three year note, so when we finally opened up, we had spent $70,000 for the whole brewery. The leasehold improvements, the wood-fired pizza oven, the kitchen, all of our furniture, our lights, the bar, and everything. So that means you can run real lean, and you don't have to charge a fortune for your product, and you can be highly profitable.

However, Molley and I were out of cash, out of credit, and out of everything but hope, and we needed money to buy the inventory to open. We were sitting at home and I said, "Hey, the flea market is tomorrow, and I bet we can get $50 bucks for our sofa, and $20 for our lights," and so on. The next day we cleared out our house of everything but our bed, and we earned around $500. We took it to Costco and bought flour, cheese, sauce ingredients, toppings, and came home with $6. We ate a dozen tacos at taco bell, and the next day we opened. Not a pretty story but we did whatever we had to. You have to believe in your dreams.

Three months after we opened we were able to replace the prep tables that we had bought cheap and fixed up ourselves, with newer and better tables. But there is still equipment to this day that we had from that day one. You know, if you buy something brand new, the day you use it it's worth pennies to the dollar, so if you can buy it used you can save on all of that devaluation.

It sounds like Tom Hennessy was a good mentor for both of you?

Yes. He has helped people all over the country. He actually has a class now where he takes people under his wing for two weeks and counsels them on how to make it work.

One important thing he told us was, "When you open up, make sure you have four products on your menu that are cheaply priced, and each ingredient on the prep table for each item must be shared by another item, so something doesn't sit there forever." He told us to keep everything simple, and unique, and to never sacrifice on quality, but to make sure to create systems that build consistency. "You don't want to hire that chef that has 20 years of experience. You want to hire somebody that has an open mind and is willing to learn it your way, but who at the same time is strong enough to tell you if he sees a better way. You've got to be flexible, and learn to adopt the good parts and ditch the bad opinions and create efficient systems."

So that's what we did. We created the pizzas exactly the way we wanted them. We took pictures of how we wanted them made in the various steps, and laminated the sheets, and we said, "This is how we want these first four pizzas made."

So you recommend finding a mentor?

Absolutely. We've seen other people go into the business, and they open up, and they are so closed minded. "I want to do it this way, and this is the only right way." Two months later, they are out of business.

Then you see other people that go in with an open mind, and say, "I am going to absorb everything I can from other people and be flexible and take the best and run with it." There are a lot of people out there that are willing to give you advice and help you out, as long as you have an open mind toward it.

You opened your second location ten years later. What was it like transitioning to owning two locations?

Everybody told us we couldn't do it, but they were the same people who told us we couldn't make it work in Socorro Springs.

We were once again looking for a small town that had similar characteristics to Socorro. I think small towns are good because you can go in there and there is the whole environment of … well there's often a bunch of people in there half-assing it. And you can go in to a town like that and come out with a product that is high quality and is professionally run, and really clean up. That's what happened when we went into Socorro.

Being in a small town made it much easier to dominate our market. If we had gone into Albuquerque and Denver, we would have to compete with national chains that have their whole system down to a science. By choosing little towns, we went against all of the conventional wisdom. You are supposed to need a much larger population than the towns we entered had. Everyone told us, "You can't do it there. It's too small." But once we started looking at the demographics, it really wasn't. It's similar to Socorro. At the same time we had a personal agenda. We wanted to be in Colorado, and in the mountains, so Buena Vista fit that.

By going into a little town like Buena Vista, you can get people excited easier. It's easy to get to know the locals quickly, and you can rapidly change your product if necessary to make them happy. For instance, we showed up in Buena Vista with the same recipes that we used in Socorro, but people in Buena Vista had different tastes. They wanted their beers to be stronger and bigger and hoppier. So we could immediately respond to that.

If you are in a large city that's hard to do. If you have a population of 2,500 locals, you can change to their tastes. If you have 100,000 locals, you can't be as flexible. Now, I recognize there are weaknesses to that strategy. If you are going to focus on small towns, you better do a great job with *all* of the locals or you're done. But I think it's easy to accomplish that, without having mass corporate chains competing with you that can compete at below cost.

How do you find people that share your passion and your desire for your business to succeed, and for your customers to be happy?

There are two answers to that. The first one is a shotgun approach. You take anybody who comes in the door because year after year it gets harder to find employees. You just take everybody and you hope one is going to work out. You hire 10 people and a year later you are only left with two of them. And the second one is you have to trust your instincts. Have you ever read the book called *Blink*?

Yes. I love Malcolm Gladwell's books.

When I was reading that book, it reminded me exactly of how we choose our employees. When someone walks in that door, right then you're thinking, "This person is perfect." Other people might sound great, or they email you their resume, and you get all excited about them, and then they walk through the door and you're thinking, "Uh-uh. This isn't gonna work."

It's a weird business. You are dealing with an interesting group of people. It's the kind of people that are either ex-professionals, and they come in with a lot of attitude – "I used to do this and this and this." While at the opposite end are people who perhaps dropped out of high school, and they kind of have a chip on their shoulder because they have been kicked around a lot.

So you have to knock down the guy with the attitude a bit, without him knowing he's getting knocked down. And then the guy who comes in with the chip on his shoulder is going to be way too defensive to let him loose with your customers, so you've gotta kind of build him up first.

But that initial impression, 90% of the time, is very telling.

What do you spend most of your time doing, as it relates to your restaurants?

It depends on where we are. When we opened Eddyline, I spent a lot of my time there. I was doing all of the beer brewing, mostly so I could perfect both the equipment and the recipes. We just hired a new brewer to take that over, which frees me up again. So then I am back to planning the next steps of our growth.

For instance, right now we're working with architects on this new building for a larger brewery. At the same time we are looking at opening another restaurant down the road in Salida. That probably takes up 30, maybe 35 hours per week.

We try to go down to our other store in New Mexico once per week, unless we have a problem with a manager or a brewer or anything else, and then we go down there more often. That takes up a good 20 hours per week.

The rest of the time is kind of broader brush management. For example, the managers might have a problem. "What do we do here?" or "This equipment broke" or "We don't know what to do about this." So you're kind of putting out fires. You're solving the problems where other people stop solving them.

That's the least enjoyable part of it. You're thinking, "These are the kinds of problems you guys should be able to solve." But everyone has a different focus. For instance, one manager has a broader brushed focus than our other manager. He'll see the bigger picture. But because of that, he won't focus in on the real small details that we need him to like the other one can. Both are great. You have to manage their strong points and not get hung up on their weaknesses, which allows them to grow stronger.

So our job is to make sure that all of the details are getting covered, and we still have a plan for growth, and we still have a plan for improving things at both locations. It's our job to make sure the smallest of the small details are getting done, and the largest of the large things are happening.

Why do you think restaurant failure rates are so high?

Molley and I talk about that all of the time. It's a lack of perspective and a lack of experience.

A lot of people that are opening restaurants have this weird perspective that their friends will come in and out all of the time. For example, we had this happen to a friend of ours. She opened up a coffee shop, thinking her friends would come, but she didn't put enough thought into how the business side was going to work.

So six months later she closed her doors saying, "I'm not making any money." I said, "Patty, I can tell from your pricing that you are not covering all of your bills and your cost of goods. You're charging $1.50 for a scone. But once you go through all of the materials and the labor and the utilities, you're cost on this scone is about $1.75. So you ought to be selling it for about $4 or $4.50 minimum if you are going to go anywhere with this."

Also, Molley and I noticed that a lot of these people who own restaurants don't eat out. We ask them where their favorite places are to go out and to have a beer, and they say, "We don't like to go out." So that's the experience part. A lot of these people don't have experience going out.

Molley and I love going out and eating and having drinks. You pick up on all of these little details. You realize that places that you don't like miss the big picture. They have this idea in their head that they are just serving the food as a product, but what they are really serving is the whole atmosphere.

Tom Hennessy wrote an awesome article about a restaurant being like an oyster. An oyster sits at the bottom of the ocean, and the tide comes in and goes out, and brings some nutrients. If the water is just right – not too murky, not too clear, it's got enough agitation. If everything is just right, it produces a pearl, and that's just like a restaurant. From the time a customer sees your restaurant and pulls into your parking lot, it's essentially that oyster. If everything goes right, at the end you will have created the pearl. You'll have a happy customer.

It has to do with how clean the parking lot is. It has to do with how clean your front door is. It has to do with lighting. I'm sure you've gone into a restaurant when it's dark outside, and you walk in and there's a flash of light, and you are just blinded. Right then, your whole mood just changed. It just transformed.

Same thing if you are coming in and it's right when the restaurant opened. Let's say it's 11:00 in the morning, and you walk in, and there's no music, and you can hear the cook's music, and you can hear the pots and pans, and you can hear the compressors in the refrigeration, and it's like this weird library. When you go into a place like that, everybody will be whispering. You know, all you have to do is turn up the music enough to cover the noise you don't want to hear, and it sets the tone. People get more upbeat. They start talking louder. Now of course when they start getting too loud you have to turn it down a bit.

You just have to pay attention to all of the details. You've got music. You've got light. You've got the general cleanliness. There's so many little details that contribute to the big picture. But if you don't have the big picture, you have nothing to go off of.

So with all of the restaurants that we've seen go out of business, we've seen those two things. One, the owners don't go out. And two, they don't have the bigger picture of what they are trying to accomplish.

What are your plans for the future?

Before we opened here in Buena Vista we had also looked at Salida. Instead of doing another brewery there, we decided to do a larger brewery here, and just a restaurant there. With a larger brewery, we are able to can our beers and distribute them.

So once we get this new brewery opened – hopefully by February, 2011 – we'll start working hard on Salida and try to have the restaurant opened by May. At that point, we're just going to try to let everything kind of run forward smoothly for a bit, and then we'll plan our next step.

Highlights – A quick recap of Mic's key points...

- ✓ Most startup books are wrong – you can start with little money

- ✓ You can dominate in small towns

- ✓ Run really lean and you can be highly profitable

- ✓ Find a mentor

- ✓ Eat at other restaurants – often

- ✓ Get all of the details right to create a pearl for your customers

Hooks, making customers feel special
& having the final say

Fudpucker's
500+ employees
Destin, FL & Ft. Walton, FL
Restaurant owner since 1983
www.fudtv.com

Chester Kroeger has owned Fudpucker's for over 30 years. He started it out of a snack bar in a nightclub, and grew it to a famous brand. Chester has found the right blend of passion and good business sense, and he's the kind of guy you'll learn something from every time you speak to him. He has been successful for several decades, and he is still as excited about his business as ever. Here's what he had to share about having hooks to draw people in, making customers feel special, why you should be the one who has the final say, and more...

How did you get started in the restaurant business?

The story changes all of the time! [Laughs] So here's my 30-year memory. My father was somewhat of an entrepreneur, and that was really the thing that set the tone for the direction I took in life.

When I went to college, I was like most people at that time. I had visions of making the world a better place. I was going to go into politics, so I studied political science and public administration. Very quickly figured out that that was not where my passion was.

The other things that I loved were music and dancing. So I sort of left politics behind and followed my passion, which I think is the key in life. That one word is probably the most important word that you could put by my name. If you're not passionate about something, there's really no point in it. Your business. Your job. Your relationships.

Where did that passion for music and dancing lead you next?

I got involved in deejay work back at the time, when John Travolta was prancing around the stage, in the disco era. I did very well with it, and the opportunity to do a restaurant actually reared its head at the nightclub where I was a disc jockey.

I wasn't actually intending to go into the restaurant business. I was more interested in opening up a bar, but the gentleman who owned the place was very frustrated one night because the guy back in the snack bar had quit. He said, "Chester, why don't you do yourself a favor, and do me a favor, and take over the snack bar?"

So the opportunity presented itself, and I took it. It was one of those defining moments. Every one of us goes past things every day that, should we choose to go in that particular direction could in fact change our life for the better or the worse.

I'm not sure the decision was based on anything other than gut. Here I am today, with two restaurants, the largest of which is around 36,000 square feet, and is an entertainment venue with food and merchandise.

Merchandise has been a big hit for you, right?

Yes, it's truly the thing that vaulted Fudpucker's from being that snack bar in the back of a local nightclub to what it is today.

I was there one night cooking, and there were a few people at the snack bar. I had four things on the menu: a "Fudburger"; a "Fishpucker"; a "Chickenpucker"; and a "Fuddog." Those were the core menu items, because that's what people wanted to eat when they were out drinking.

One of the guys was just absolutely hammered. He placed his order, and as he was kind of leaning there on the bar, he said, "Why don't you do a t-shirt? With a name like Fudpucker's, you'd make a million dollars." And it gelled. It was almost instantaneous. It was another one of those moments that you have to seize. We made these shirts, and put them up for sale, and they sold very quickly. Almost immediately. We started selling four, five, six, eight a night from the snack bar.

I wanted to get more exposure for my shirt, and meanwhile, the owner of the club was having a terrible time selling the club shirts. He was smart to put some pretty girls behind the booth, but they didn't have the right incentive and they didn't have the right attitude. So I approached him, and asked, "Can I put some energy into this? Maybe train your people, and put some of my shirts up here." He said, "Sure."

Maybe I should have told him this, but I told the girls, "If you sell one of my shirts, I'll give you $0.50." Obviously they had incentive to sell my shirt, and it worked. We ripped through hundreds and hundreds of shirts. It was very successful. When you think about it being in just the one location, and the word started getting out – people started coming just to buy the shirt. That was the beginning of Fudpucker's.

How did that evolve into starting a restaurant?

About a year later, I heard about a place called "The Deck" that was for rent on the beach east of Destin. It had been operated for years by a young hippie dude. Great guy.

His concept was selling shark. Shark on a stick. Shark burgers. You name it. That was back in the time when "Jaws" was in the movies, and people were kinda focused on that. Why not eat some shark?

Well, the only problem was that he caught them on the same beach where his restaurant was located. He'd have these lines out there, and at night he'd catch the sharks. He'd bring them up and he'd leave the carcass on the beach. [Laughs]

People were freaking out, saying, "I'm not gonna swim there." He started wondering why his business was failing. Well, the whole thing was based on people walking up from the beach and grabbing a shark burger or whatever. So, needless to say, he lost the business.

So you saw an opportunity?

Yes. It wasn't a nice restaurant. It was a shack on the beach. But the girl I was dating had a friend who knew the people that owned the property. She put me in touch with them, and we struck a deal on a lease.

The lease was from May 15 through September 15, which is the prime season along the Gulf Coast. I didn't have to pay anything the other months – I just paid for those four months in the summer. It was a ridiculous rent. I look back on it and think, well, I wish those deals existed today. And truthfully, in the economy that we're in right now, they may.

Tell me about getting started. What worked for you?

We opened Fudpucker's in 1983 in that location, and it was an immediate success. The t-shirts are the thing that carried it. I think that's because in this day and age, you almost have to have a hook. The hook can be anything, but it has to increase your sales. There has to be a reason for people to come to see you. If you don't have that, then why would they choose you over another place?

I had absolutely no formal restaurant training whatsoever. I was again just going by my gut, and my ability to cook, which was decent. The success of that place, in my opinion, was quite phenomenal.

The sales started doubling. And then they would quadruple. It just went nuts. Eventually, we opened up another location in Ft. Walton Beach, because I knew that I was going to have to leave that location. The owners knew about the success I was having, and didn't like it. I guess they wanted to try it on their own. So we moved from there to Ft. Walton, and then a couple or three years later we opened up a store in Destin.

So hooks can be a great business driver?

Yes. In the Destin store, we built what we call a trading company, which not only sells t-shirts, but also other Fudpucker branded material. Hats. Cups. Glasses. Magnets. You name it. Then we took it a step further, and we made it an actual gift shop. It's a real shopping experience, and that has been one of the things that I would consider as our hook.

Do you have other hooks?

Yes. A few years after we built the gift shop, we were trying to generate more business during the day. Like most beach locations, people tend to go to the beach during the day hours. As such, your lunch business is not as strong as your dinner, and we were trying to figure out a way to get the day business. Man, we tried everything. We threw a lot of time and passion into trying to come up with something that would work.

Finally, my three partners and I were at a restaurant show down in Orlando and we saw a booth with everything from fish to turtles ... basically stuffed things. The owner, Gerald, was a fascinating guy. He had been an alligator wrestler in an earlier life. He was also Special Forces in the Army, and a Mr. Florida in the middle weight class.

He started talking about what he did, and the more he talked, the more intrigued we got about incorporating some of the things that he had in his booth in our restaurant. It came up that we had a pond in front of the restaurant, and he said, "You might want to just think about putting alligators in that pond." We laughed it off.

He said, "Yeah, and let me tell you why. What are the two things that people really come to Florida to see? And I'll give you a hint. Neither one is the beach. And they're both animals." We eventually guess Disney, which he confirmed was the number one reason people come to Florida. They come to see the mouse. He said the second thing they come to see is the alligators. He told us he couldn't give us a mouse, but he could give us an alligator exhibit, and he could make it something that people really enjoy.

The light went on for another hook?

Yes, the light went on. We recognized the potential for that. So we ended up creating an exhibit we call "Alligator Beach." Amazingly enough, over the next year, our sales during the day quadrupled. Largely because we became a location for people to take their families, and not just look at alligators, but get educated about them, feed them and hold one and have a picture taken.

I give a great deal of credit to Gerald for training my son, Brand – who was at the time 14 years of age, and who is now in officer candidate school. He actually took that business by the horns, at the young age of 14, and created the script that is still used today – with some very minor modifications – and put his life into it. He put his whole being into it. He became known as The Gator Guy. The success of that little element of Fudpucker's continues to this day.

Why is it so important to have a hook to draw people in?

The point of having a hook is to increase the reasons for people to come to you. Why would they come to you? Well, it can be a great hamburger. It can be a great steak. It can be a super drink. It can be a t-shirt. Or it can be something else. You have to choose what you want. But I also honestly believe that you need more than just good food in today's world. People look to be entertained, and entertainment comes in a variety of ways. It can be as simple as building a circular bar in your restaurant, where people can sit around it and make eye contact. This was popularized a lot of years ago by Applebee's and T.G.I. Friday's and a lot of other places. And there's a reason for that: People become the entertainment. People come there to be entertained by others.

The concept of a really stunning drink can be a hook. We have a Voodoo Magic, and a Fudpucker Punch, and a Big Blue Margarita.

The Big Blue Margarita is a 40-ounce margarita served in a martini-type glass. When it goes through the crowd, people go, "Oh my God. I have to have one of those. What is that?" When you serve it, the whole table gets up and sticks a straw in it and all drink it at the same time, and it creates an event.

It's the same thing with fajitas. I mean, think about it. Why would you buy low grade meat, sliced thin? Well, it's the sizzle. Look, there's nothing wrong with fajitas. I love them. But the reason to buy them is the sizzle. It's the plate they come out on. It's steaming and sizzling and you can hear it coming. It grabs people's attention. "Oh my God, I want one of those!"

Same thing with putting food out on the table. When you come here for a hamburger, you get a hamburger. I mean, it's more than a mouthful. And we do that with everything. We do that with every item that's on our menu. We try to make it bigger than life. It's definitely not cheap.

Do you offer specially-priced items?

Yes, we do have some bargain things, especially during day parts when we need to produce more traffic. Economic times like these demand that you have some value-priced items. But you know, you engineer those so that those actually make you money.

I fail to understand why restaurants will sell something for cost. It just doesn't make sense. All you are doing is devaluing everything else. So a recommendation I would have is to price your product so that you can make something off of it.

You can engineer a piece of fish a thousand ways to make it profitable. What do you pair it with? How big of a portion is it? What kind of a sauce do you put on it? Do you put a sauce on it? What do you serve it on? There are a million things you can do to make that attractive and cost effective, and still something that people would recognize as a bargain, while you're still making money.

What's an example?

We have a lot of things on our menu right now that are $7.99 to $9.99. You'd think that it's hard to make any money like that, especially when you're serving them a full meal. But that's not the case at all. Yes, we're making less when someone orders that, but that person, who's on a budget, may not have come here unless we had something in that price range.

How important is good service?

Very important! So far we've covered everything from the necessity to have passion, to having a hook, to wowing your customer, which is really the key to success. You put passion together with a product that people just can't seem to be without, and you've got a really good chance of success, even if you're a moderately intelligent business person.

But I think one of the other key factors is service. Together with wanting to be entertained, customers today go out because they want to be treated special. They want to be served. They want to be taken care of. They want to feel like they matter. If you fail at any point in the course of the service experience, you will likely have lost a customer, and potentially many more. If a person has a bad experience at your restaurant, they're going to probably tell 10 people. Conversely, if they have a great experience, they might tell two or three. That's just the way it is.

We focus heavily on service. Two years ago, we made a dramatic shift. Not that we were doing a bad job with service, but it seemed to me as if we had lost the importance of it in our training. And we were, in my opinion, accepting mediocrity from the line staff.

It was a management thing. There were so many other restaurants opening, and all of these places were offering big money, and the opportunity for advancement, and corporate world kind of stuff. A lot of people – good servers, good cooks, and all of these good people that we had had over the years – were lured by that. Now an awful lot of those places are no longer in business, but that's another story.

So you had a hard time keeping people?

I guess what I'm saying is that we reduced our standards. We just didn't feel like we could compete, and I was wrong. I should have seen it immediately, but thankfully, a couple of years back, we were able to recognize it.

Now, our motto is "Never accept mediocrity." The standing order to all of our managers is that, regardless of how good your staff is, there's always one, or two, or three that could use improvement. You are to constantly hire and replace those people who you feel are less deserving or who don't cut it.

I understand you have a performance-based culture.

Yes, that sounds kind of harsh. Not settling for mediocrity means that everyone on your staff knows that they have to perform in just about every aspect. They can't come into work disheveled. They have to be groomed properly. They can't be wearing dirty clothes – we have certain standards. All those things have to be met.

You know, all of these things can affect the way a customer perceives their service. In addition to that, they have a smile on their face at all times. Their work is their work. They leave their personal problems at home. They don't talk about their issues in the wait station.

In fact, if anything, they're not supposed to be in the wait station at all, except to get drinks for customers or service items that are necessary for the tables. We ask them to stay in the dining rooms, so they can be aware of customer needs. There's nothing like being in a restaurant, and you're enjoying your meal, and you run out of sweet tea. O.K., well you really want to have some more of that food, but you really want to have some tea to wash it down, and you can't seem to get anybody's attention. Pretty quickly your whole perception changes. The point is, the waiters and waitresses stay in the dining rooms, and they are constantly vigilant.

How are they vigilant?

When they take an order, they do it professionally. They write everything down. I don't believe in these restaurants where the customer gets impressed with a waiter who has a table of six and he takes everybody's order, and he does it mentally. That is impressive, but there's always that question in the back of my mind: "Is this guy going to screw up my order?" And it happens on occasion, so we make our staff write down the orders. People feel more assured. They feel more comfortable.

We also check with them constantly, throughout the course of their meal. Not only does the waiter do it, but the busboys do it. And there's a standing rule at our restaurant that managers must visit the table at least once during the dining experience.

You expect a lot of your staff, but I know you treat them very well.

Absolutely. Our employees know that they're appreciated, perhaps more so than in any other places I've been associated with. We treat our people with respect. We demand a lot from them, but when they achieve what they set out to achieve, they get rewarded.

It's not just the money that they make. It's the way they're treated by the managers and by the owners. We have become somewhat of a big family. At the peak of our season Fudpucker's has 500 employees. That's the two stores and some of the affiliated businesses, and back office. I cannot tell you that I know everybody's name, but I do my very best to acknowledge the core people, or the people who I know for any length of time, who are stellar performers.

We recently had a little employee appreciation party, and we had a blast. It was an end of the summer thing. About 60 people showed up. Even though I couldn't hang until 2:00 or 3:00 in the morning like these guys do, I was there until 11:30 or 12:00. We just had a great time. In fact, somebody told me there's a video on YouTube of me dancing. It's an ugly sight, I can assure you. [Laughs]

How else do you create a great work atmosphere?

You also listen to your staff. That's an absolute necessity. A lot of owners of restaurants feel like they know everything, and I've been victim of that too. You have a certain amount of success in life, and all of a sudden, you're invincible. Well, trust me, that's not the case. You can always learn, and who better to learn from than the person who is having contact with your customers every single day?

We regularly have opportunities for our employees to let us know what we should be doing, or to express their concerns. We do it in a variety of ways. We have meetings. We have comment boxes. We have a standing policy that if someone comes up with an idea that we use – for a drink, or for a different way of serving something, or a new item, or whatever – then we give them a bonus.

So we have a lot of interaction with our staff, and that also goes to the appreciation factor. There's very little that you can do that's more important than lend an ear to what someone else is saying to you. It's like, "Wow! He really wants to know." Not all of the ideas are out there. They may not get picked up. But sometimes something comes along that'll just rock your world. That happens quite a bit, actually.

How about an example?

I was reluctant to change the menu this year, for a variety of reasons. I wanted to focus on cost savings. But I've got a young man who is a new manager for us, and he had an idea to do a themed menu for lunches. Not only did he have the idea, but he had the ability and the guts to step up and create it, with the help of some of our kitchen crew. They refined this menu to the point where – I guess it was a week or so ago – they invited us to lunch at Fudpucker's, and provided this absolutely amazing country-style meal. It was very different than what we do. We don't do country meals typically – it's more of an American bistro kind of place with a very heavy push towards seafood.

I was absolutely blown away by the quality, by the presentation, by the quantity, and by the fact that this guy had taken it from conception all the way through to presentation. So next time you're over this way, you can enjoy a country fried steak, with mashed red potatoes and gravy, a fried grit cake with bacon, cheese, onion, garlic, and red bell pepper infused, and a beautiful side dish of either fresh corn, or green beans with stewed tomatoes.

172

So Paul is going to get a nice little reward for this. Especially if it takes off, which I think it will.

How important is it to have efficient operations?

You have to have a very strong back of the house. You have to have an excellent program for dealing with inventory. Poor inventory management can kill you. You have to have a very strong program for being able to manage the menu. If you don't adequately or accurately price things, you're not going to be in business long. Whether it's overpriced, or underpriced. Either way, you could lose.

Timely reporting is critical as well. It doesn't really do you a whole lot of good when the information you're getting is a week or a month late. God help you if it's more than a month late. How can you make decisions about tomorrow, when you don't have the facts about today? You can't expect to have a financial statement prepared every day. It's impossible. I don't care how many bookkeepers you have. But you can have some reports that talk about theoretical food costs or where your labor is as a percentage of last year, or as a percentage of your sales. And I'm being very simple here – it gets very technical, but the bottom line is that we review our labor every day. We look at it historically, not just over one year, but over a two- or three-year period.

And we look at our cost of sales. We have a person on our management team that does virtually nothing other than buying. We can do that because we're a big operation, but even a small operator has got to stay on top of his pricing that he gets from vendors. You know, these guys are out to make money. The best way to keep these folks honest is to make sure they are competing with someone else.

So your back of the house has to be a well-oiled machine. It has to provide you with the information needed to provide the absolute best quality, at the best price, for your customer.

Do you make seasonal purchases to hedge your seafood costs?

Yes, we lock in prices on large quantities of a product. Whether it be fish, or shrimp, or ground beef … all things that are the core elements of our business. We try to find the best time of the year to buy them. You don't want to try to buy Alaskan snow crab in August, because the season is over. It's been over for months, and you're going to pay through the nose for that product. You buy it when they're catching the crab or shrimp or Mahi-Mahi or other types of fish. You try to lock in your pricing, and take advantage of bulk buying.

Restaurant partnerships fail a lot. What makes them work?

My philosophy is that somebody has to be in control. I think 50/50 partnerships never work, unless it is a unique relationship. Those things are subject to change. Why would you have someone in your business that can basically block anything you want to do or say? I would never do that.

I've always brought in partners. I do it regularly. When we have a manager who's running a store, we typically offer him a percentage of ownership. But they're never at my level. I won't do it. I trust myself. If I go off the deep end, I guess that's my choice. [Laughs]

The reality is that somebody has to be able to say, "This is the way it's gonna be." That avoids a lot of problems with partners. You try your very best to present your case, so that you win them over to your way of opinion, but it doesn't always work that way. There are some times over the course of our 30 odd years in business that we've had insurmountable differences … very seldom, but it does happen. And I'm still here, so the business is still here.

What do you hope the future holds for your restaurants?

Well, honestly, this has been the most difficult year (2010) that I think I've ever had, and it was only because of the BP oil spill. Restaurants throughout this part of Florida were severely affected by the fact that people did not come here. They were scared of oil on the beach. They didn't want to eat the seafood.

So the future for right now is getting through the next nine months, so that I can get into my core season next year. Every ounce of my being is focused on getting enough money from outside sources, because BP sure isn't paying the tab. They haven't given us anything. We have a little over a million dollars worth of claims in with them right now. And that number is going to increase. But we haven't seen a dime. Business is down anywhere between 17% to 35%. On average. Sometimes it's been down over 50%.

Fudpucker's is currently looking for venture money. We think that part of the way to get out of the current situation is to expand our operations. We have some very good locations picked out in markets like Panama City, and Pensacola Beach, and even further east, and further west.

So that's where we're focused. We would love to take this concept and bring it to several other locations along the Gulf Coast in the next five to 10 years. But the key is getting through the next nine months. I think that as long as we continue to provide the great service, and the good food, and wow our customers, then we should do fine. It's just a blip on the radar right now. The times are what they are, and the strong will survive.

Highlights – A quick recap of Chester's key points...

- ✓ Have a hook to draw people in

- ✓ Offer bargains, but not without a profit

- ✓ Make your customers feel special

- ✓ Reward successful ideas

- ✓ Timely reporting is critical

- ✓ Own more than 50% of your restaurant

*Passion, planning
& serving from the heart*

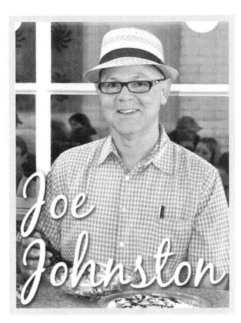

Joe's Real BBQ
Liberty Market
Joe's Farm Grill

125+ employees
Gilbert, AZ
Restaurant owner since 1989
www.joesrealbbq.com
www.libertymarket.com
www.joesfarmgrill.com

Joe Johnston has been building highly successful restaurants for more than 20 years. After co-founding and later selling a chain of coffee shops in Arizona called The Coffee Plantation, Joe has helped build three incredibly popular restaurants in Gilbert, AZ. He and his partners build institutions - restaurants that won't be replicated and will be around for many years to come. Joe has a proven track record of success, and has figured out how to mitigate most of the risks that come along with opening restaurants. Speaking to him is like speaking to somebody who turns everything he touches to gold...

How did you get started in the restaurant industry?

I grew up here in Gilbert on a family farm. That's now the Agritopia Community [a housing community built around an urban farm], and it's also where we have Joe's Farm Grill.

I went to the Naval Academy in Annapolis for a couple of years, and then decided the Navy wasn't for me. Then I attended Stanford for four years, and graduated with degrees in electrical and mechanical engineering, and a Masters in Engineering Management. I did engineering for a company for two years, and then I did consulting engineering with my own company for about five years.

But I've always been interested in food, and interested in people and socializing. So my business partner, Tim, and I were in a small group at church. We enjoyed one another, and our wives enjoyed one another, and we thought that some day it would be fun to go into business together. And we'd occasionally do some sort of hobby activities, like maybe cooking.

One month we decided to experiment with coffee. We learned how to roast coffee at our house, and that was an exciting thing to learn. We started thinking that maybe coffee would be a good business to start.

When I went to Stanford, there were coffee houses all around campus. I thought maybe there were none in Arizona because it's so darn hot, and maybe nobody would want to have coffee in a hot climate. But then we went down to a coffee shop in Tucson, close to the university, and noticed that it was really busy. We then went to Flagstaff, in Northern Arizona, and Macy's [European Coffee House] was up there. They'd already been in business for eight years, and they were busy. So we started thinking that maybe we had no coffee shops near us simply because no one had done it.

We decided to start researching it. One of the things that we always try to do is to do a lot of research. Go and visit some of the best people who are doing something, and see if you can get a half hour's time out of them. Observe their businesses. Write down what you like, and what you don't like. Even go to some bad places. Almost every bad place has some good things about it, and you can also learn some things not to do.

We went up and down the California coast, and looked and saw what was being done. Then we ended up looking for locations, and developing the concept for what we wanted to do, which was going to include roasting coffee. We found a location by Arizona State University, which is one of the top two or three largest universities in the country. The location was on Mill Avenue, which at the time was a slowly redeveloping, ramshackle area headed toward revitalization.

We opened a 2,700 square foot place. We decided that because it wasn't New York City, we couldn't just do coffee. Instead, we realized we needed a broad enough concept that we can make enough money, so we added quality baked goods. We decided to do kitchen food, retail and roasting.

Tell me about getting started.

We started out in 1989, and it was busy off the bat. Then it started getting really busy, so I started looking for another location.

I found a planter in the middle of the section of the Scottsdale Fashion Square, in front of Neiman Marcus. I proposed to the developer to replace that planter with a round kiosk. That became our second store.

We started selling wholesale to restaurants and grocery stores, and build a roasting plant. By '92 we did another large scale coffee house at Biltmore Fashion Park. By that same time, our original store was doing about $2,250,000 with an average ticket of $2.25. So that's about one million people in one year in one store. It was crazy busy, and the company was getting bigger and bigger. We had 150 employees.

An overnight success!

Yes, but I was beginning to get really dissatisfied, because my basic gift is creativity, but I was spending a lot of my time on things like personnel issues. I love people, but I really don't like that kind of thing, so I was starting to feel really caged in, and not really liking my work. It's kind of bad when you create your own prison.

Tim and I decided that we would put the company up for sale, because we didn't see any other way out of it. Maybe in retrospect, hiring some professional management, or doing some other things probably would have made sense. But we just decided to sell.

We sold the company via a local company that did mergers and acquisitions, and they hooked us up with Second Cup from Canada. We sold The Coffee Plantation to them, and Tim and I had a two-year employment contracts.

We built an additional 16 stores in the next two years. I went from being pretty busy and not that happy, to being really busy, and not necessarily that happy. As a creative person, having to rush through and build so much stuff, without a good underpinning, was very difficult.

In that time frame though, they built stores in Texas and California, and more in Arizona. At that time, when I was in Texas, I got to see barbecue in a serious way. I was already thinking, "What am I going to do after this?" and it stuck in my mind that barbecue and the coffee business were similar.

It's a broad demographic. Everybody loves barbecue. Almost everybody loves coffee. It's a single product, single process business. So you have the coffee roaster for coffee. And you have the smoker for barbecue. If you can really understand your process, and keep controls over the factors in that one process, then that's good. And you can also be known for something. I think sometimes with the broadline restaurants, it's hard for people to put a finger on why they're special, or what they're known for.

I also liked how they're both very social places. Places where people can just get together and meet and socialize over food. I also like the simplicity of both operations. Barbecue is relatively straightforward and understandable, and coffee is straightforward and understandable.

So that is kind of a nutshell between starting The Coffee Plantation, and having the first inkling of Joe's Real Barbecue.

Do you think you do more planning before starting your restaurants than most people do?

Well, let me tell you why I'm so keen on planning and the proper fit of people's giftedness. After I left The Coffee Plantation, I decided to take a one-year sabbatical to reflect on what I was good at, what I enjoyed doing, and about life in general. With clarity of mind, I realized I am a fairly narrowly gifted idea person, but I am an idea person that gets ideas converted into reality.

So I started to see that as an entrepreneur. I think that sometimes there is the idea that the American dream is independence, and being the self-made man who can do it alone, a good entrepreneur has the whole package. Well, the fact is that generally nobody has the whole package. I think from a biblical perspective, that certainly is the case. There's the idea of people with different gifts working together to accomplish something.

I decided that going forward, I would do what I'm good at and not get involved in things like management and the other stuff that caused my undoing in terms of lack of fulfillment and happiness with The Coffee Plantation. I was going to take care of ideas and concepts, and get them rolling, but find a partner or partners with the same vision and passion to cover the operating side.

So for me personally, interdependence, rather than independence, has been incredibly freeing. The main thing is that you just have to make sure that your partners are – almost as in a marital situation – on the same page. That was something that really crystallized in my mind – that I needed to work on just being a creative person, and a head cheerleader for other people, to drive these things home. So my experience with barbecue has been much, much better because I have stuck to that assiduously.

Also, as a creative person, I decided that I was going to enjoy the design and creation process. Because, for a creative person, what else is there? The process is as enjoyable as the end product. Since I'm a low-risk person, I've got to make sure that as I go down that process, that this is a reasonable risk to take. Restaurants are traditionally thought of as risky ventures. I don't necessarily consider them risky at all if you do them correctly, but I have to get to that point where I feel it's not that risky.

The creative process is critical for you.

Yes, the creative process for me is huge. Research is only one phase of the creative process. In the creative process, you have to create a library in your mind of images and experiences that you can draw from when you create things. There's no such thing as a completely novel, completely new idea. The more you travel, the more knowledge you gain, the better.

What I call it is the "first creation." The creation in your mind or on paper. That first creation is so important, but so many people short change it. The second creation, which is actually doing it physically – building the building, the equipment, the menu, etc. – and actually making stuff, is never better than the first.

So if you haven't spent the time in the first creation, richly enjoying it, and embellishing it, and building layers of reasons why people will want to come, and building the story, then the second creation is just going to be half-cocked. And why bother? There's only a couple of reasons why people might want to come, and you're going to take shortcuts. You're going to open discombobulated. Why?

So for me, those two things are a big deal. First, know your giftedness, and put together a team of complimentary gifts with the same goal. Second, take time to do the first creation right, before you launch into the second creation.

These two things are how you mitigate your risks and set yourself up for the best chance of success?

That's my goal. Since The Coffee Plantation, our end game has been something very different than before. I assumed The Coffee Plantation was going to go on for a long time, and actually it still exists under other ownership, but much scaled down.

Our intention since then has been to build institutions, where the end game is not to build a unit and sell it, or build up a chain and sell it. Our basic end game is no end game. The idea is, we're trying to build something that's going to last. The single unit economics just have to work. Ours is a very old fashioned technique, which is to build a great store, and run it well, and it's got to be nicely profitable. It's got to be designed to be livable for the managers. It's got to be designed to be livable for the employees. There's got to be benefits. There's got to be stability, and that sort of thing.

Did you borrow money to start any of your places?

No. I'm a no-debt person.

Is it a bad idea to take on debt?

No, it's not a bad idea at all, but it just increases the risk.

It's like at The Coffee Plantation. For us to get the original location, we didn't have to go into any debt for it. But to actually convince the landlord – on his brand new, multi-million dollar project with a fairly high-profile developer – that we should get the prime space? We had to have a really good business plan for them to give us the prime space when they wanted a national tenant in there. They had to believe in us to give us that space, instead of a space that we might have died in.

So I really think somebody that has to seek out financing, needs to have a really solid business plan, and a good first creation. That's how you can demonstrate to people, whether they be bankers, relatives or whoever, that you have put in the time and effort and thought to develop a concept, and a menu, and a floor plan that makes sense ... and that it's low risk on their part as well.

I do a lot of free mentoring of people that bug me until I say, "Yeah, I'll mentor you, but so long as you do this, this and this." With the young people that I mentor, I always have them go through that first creation and do the business plan.

So it doesn't freak them out, I don't lay out the whole thing at once. Every two weeks, I say, "O.K., now you're gonna write this section." I kind of lead them down the pathway bit by bit, so they don't become frightened. The whole task can seem overwhelming, but if you break it up into pieces, it's certainly doable.

What is the secret sauce that has helped you build "institutions"?

We just try to do two things: A) have a passion for food, and B) serve people from the heart. We try to keep it really simple.

If you have a passion for food, you're going to use professional preparation and training. It's going to be a clean place. You're going to be looking for great flavor profiles. You're not going to rest on your laurels. You're not going to become passionless about food, and start making boring, chain-style food.

And serving from the heart is really important. You're not serving for money, or for personal glory. You genuinely enjoy serving people, and that again drives good decision-making at the ownership level and at the brigade level. Given any decision making, you ask, "Is this serving us? Or is this serving from the heart?"

So our owners should serve our brigade members from the heart, and almost put them above customers, because the brigade members are the ones that serve nearly all of the customers. So if you don't serve your brigade members from the heart, then that kind of rings hollow that they should serve from the heart.

That's definitely simple: Have a passion for food, and serve from the heart.

Yes, and combined with those two points, we do try to create very unique places. All three restaurants are very unique, and they all have stories. We build layers of true stories. These aren't things like you find at chain restaurants, where they're talking about some character that doesn't exist, and making up all of these random stories that aren't connected to anything.

All of ours are anchored in fact, like the age of the buildings, and that they're all buildings that have been something else. Joe's Farm Grill was my house. Joe's Real BBQ was a grocery store, and several other things since then. Liberty Market has been a grocery store since 1935. There's a lot of history built in there, and then we try to layer in additional stories, in terms of the food, and why we do what we do, and where we get products from.

How do you find people that have a passion for food, and want to serve from the heart?

Well you can tell if people are "people-people" or not pretty quickly. And obviously we hire on a trial period, to see if they're able to do the things that we would like to see.

One group I like to hire from are people who are customers who love the place. They already understand the atmosphere. They already understand the feel of the place. They kind of fall in love with it, and they want to be a part of it. That's usually a no-brainer.

We also work very carefully to make sure that when we hire, the interviews involve two or three people. We try to make sure that we all agree that the personality is a good fit, and then we can train skills. But I think personality is already set by the time they come by our place.

Sadly, for example, in hiring at the espresso bar at Liberty Market, I've had to not hire some really, really, incredibly gifted baristas. They met criteria one, which is that they were crazy passionate about coffee, but they were not that passionate about people. I can't have someone who's passionate about an inanimate object, but not passionate about the people they're serving.

You have partners that manage the day-to-day stuff. How do you spend most of your time?

I've structured mine so that I have no employees, which is very handy. It enables a creative person to enjoy the things they've created, but I don't feel constrained by personnel issues. I can enjoy the brigade members. I can enjoy interacting with them, and I really love them. But I don't have to deal with it when they're late, and all of that sort of stuff.

Once something is started, then I am there to help make sure that it stays on track. Also, one of the things that's dangerous as an institution is the idea of resting on your laurels, and not being in a state of constant improvement. I am always looking at projects that I can do within those operations to move them forward. Projects that are hard for the operator to do because they are working on the day-to-day operations.

For example, I am working on a mini-business plan for Joe's Real BBQ on a mobile unit, and another one to make the restaurant's catering business more proactive. At Joe's Farm Grill, I'm working on converting the small wares from all disposable to a different approach, while also creating an outdoor catering venue. At Liberty

Market, I'm working on the beer and wine program as well as converting one part of the building from marketplace to another use.

We also have a commercial corner here at Agritopia, and I'm working on a very large scale, 25- to 30-acre project to make our corner the epicenter of food experience in Arizona. I'm trying to design it so that we get a bunch of restaurateurs in here that I like, and that have the criteria of, first of all, being passionate. And second, of knowing their craft. And third, of being very focused on quality ingredients. I'd like to plug those people into sort of a food network row in our area.

Highlights – A quick recap of Joe's key points...

✓ Visit people who are already doing something similar to what you're planning

✓ Freedom comes from interdependence

✓ Restaurants don't have to be risky

✓ Take time to perfect and enjoy your first creation

✓ Hire people who are passionate about both food and people

Social media, unconventional wisdom & building institutions

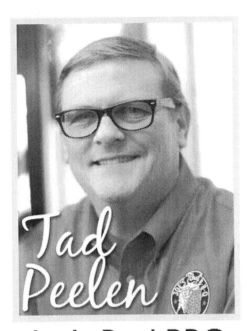

Joe's Real BBQ
Joe's Farm Grill
100+ employees
Gilbert, AZ
Restaurant owner since 1998
www.joesrealbbq.com
www.joesfarmgrill.com

Like many folks getting into the restaurant business, Tad made a switch after a career in a different field. He was in corporate communications at American Airlines for 17 years prior to helping start Joe's Real BBQ. Tad talked about unraveling his corporate mindset, the dilemma of debt, the value of technology and how to retain great people. He's done an amazing job over the last 12 years of helping turn both restaurants into institutions that are loved by their customers and admired by their peers. Here's what Tad had to say...

How did you get involved in the restaurant business?

I have two business partners. My brother Tim, and Joe Johnston. They contacted me when I was with American Airlines in their headquarters in Dallas, TX, negotiating labor agreements. I had spent 17 years at the airline, and then got this phone call about going into the restaurant business.

It was intriguing because it was an opportunity to move home. I grew up here. My folks were here. I had family here. I was getting to go into business with my brother. And it was intriguing to get back into the restaurant business.

I had cut my teeth in the restaurant business, starting when I was 14, so it was a neat opportunity to get back into the business. The fact that it was as a business partner and co-owner made it even cooler.

So my wife and I and our children packed up, and moved to Gilbert, AZ. We opened our doors on January 20, 1998, and have been serving good barbecue ever since. We opened Joe's Farm Grill in 2006 with the same partner group.

Was it tough to transition from a gigantic corporation to a startup restaurant?

Well, I was surprised along the way at a whole bunch of things that I hadn't counted on. I came in with expectations that were perhaps unrealistic.

For instance, I thought that if you took the 27-page employee manual and had it translated to Spanish, the resulting Spanish manual would be an awesome tool for every Spanish-speaking employee on your payroll. I spent thousands of dollars and had everything translated, only to find that most of my Spanish-only speaking employees weren't going to benefit much from that. The whole written thing wasn't doing much for them anyways. They learned verbally. They learned by being shown.

So when you have this corporate mindset that you can fix everything with money, or you can fix everything if you look at it correctly – that truly turned out not to be the case. I needed to get in my employees' shoes and figure out what was going to work best for them. It's not always the same as it is in the corporate world.

How far along in the planning process were you brought in?

I was brought in toward the end. I was fully employed with American Airlines, and I was just starting to sever my relationship with them. I was trying to strike a deal where I could do some consulting, which I did. I actually didn't sever my ties for quite a few years.

When we decided to open Joe's Farm Grill, our second concept, it gave me an opportunity to be involved at every stage of the process. We traveled the country finding unique independent restaurants that were doing things well, and some doing things we hoped to avoid. We knew we had to do something very unique given the location and history of the place [in Joe's childhood home next to a working urban farm].

What issues were top of mind before you opened?

Some of the things that were top of mind are probably top of mind for everyone who is in that position. "We've invested all of this money. How do you calculate break even? What does that look like? When are we going to see it? At what point do we think we'll be profitable?" Everybody goes through those calculations.

We were thinking about having the best possible tools to give our employees the best possible chance of success. With independents, I think that is one of the places where people tend to perhaps fall short. For example, if you're a chain operator and you're opening store number 742, then you send out the team, and you send out the manual. It's all been written for you. The beauty of it is, you do it just like you did at store 741.

We didn't have that luxury. We had to take everything we wanted to make happen, and determine how. So with the first time you do anything, there's great fear and trepidation. What are our policies regarding this? What do benefits look like? What do benefits cost?

I think all of those things are common to all startups. But I think the thing we thought about — that perhaps not all startups think about at the inception stage — is that we very much endeavored from well before we opened to create an institution. We didn't just want a restaurant. We didn't want a great family restaurant. We didn't want a place that most people liked. We wanted to create an institution.

So we struggled with questions about whether that approach was prideful, boastful, realistic or even smart. Ultimately, we undoubtedly wanted to create an institution, a place that you would feel you must take people to when they come in from out of town. A place that endures. A place that has longevity. A place that will be there after 10, 20, even 50 years.

We were not out to create a successful business that could be sold for a lot of money. Rather, we were out to create a successful business so that we could pass it along to other generations, and ensure the institution is still an institution after we're gone.

When did you start to believe you had achieved that goal?

I don't know that there's a single answer. We'd probably say we had accomplished that on our tenth anniversary. But I'd like to think that the answer is held by others, and not us. Are newspapers writing that you're an institution? Are bloggers indicating that you have to go to this place when you have out-of-town guests? And, in fact, by the time we had hit our fifth birthday or so, that was happening.

At 10 years, I think we felt comfortable looking at each other and saying, "I think we accomplished that goal." When you Google us, and you see what people are saying, that's what they're saying. They're saying we're the place you have to take your friends and family from out of town. In fact, they use that word, "institution." It was cool to kind of have that confirmed for us.

That was an ambitious goal. What did you do to help make it happen?

We didn't let conventional wisdom play much of a role in our decision making.

We're Christian guys who meet every week, and pray for our employees by name before we start our partner meetings. And we leave those things to Him. It's either going to thrive or die. It's really out of our hands. What we're tasked with doing is making good decisions that are in the best interest of our customers and our employees.

196

For instance, we thought early on that we probably couldn't afford health insurance for our employees. So we thought about it, and prayed about it, and we said, "You know what? It's the right thing to do for these employees, so we're going to do it. If it's successful, it's going to accomplish the goal of retaining those people who came to work here for that reason."

It was pretty uncommon in 1998 in Gilbert, AZ, for people to offer a full package to hourly restaurant employees – employees who in many cases were making slightly over the minimum. So we paid more than the norm, then we threw a benefits package on top of it.

Over the years we have sought to add more benefits, like a 401K retirement plan with matching, paid birthdays off, paid time off, and anniversary bonuses so we could treat our part-time employees as well as the full timers.

We think that's part of how you become an institution. Institutions are places that people come to eat where they see familiar faces serving them. They see familiar managers. They see familiar owners walking around the place. If we had any shot at retaining people in the long term, and having a truly fulfilled, happy, vibrant work force, it was going to take making some decisions that weren't necessarily initially in the best economic interest of the three of us.

What social media tools do you use, and how does it help your business?

We started with Twitter, added Facebook shortly thereafter, and more recently started employing Foursquare. It helps our business in a few ways. Most importantly, it has allowed us to put many more names with faces, or avatars, of our customers. When we see someone tweeting a photo of their lunch, we can make sure we get by the table and make a personal connection. We made personal connections before, but these interactions initiated by happy diners are really fun and lead to interesting conversations.

Facebook users are awesome and passionate about places they frequent. We offer a generous Mayor incentive on Foursquare (a free meal), and love seeing people talk about how they want to knock the current Mayor off their perch.

As trite as it sounds, the "social" part of social media allows us to make more personal connections and relationships. We think the time investment is worth every minute.

How do you find the right people to be a part of your team?

There is no single great answer. My best answers and best suggestions are imperfect. Nonetheless, we think based on the tenure of our folks we've probably done a relatively good job of finding great people, and perhaps an even better job of keeping those people around.

The soft economy has brought with it a silver lining in terms of the available labor pool. We've moved from having very few people to interview to having a thick stack of applications on file at any given time. This lets us take our time and be very deliberate. We don't hire anyone without two interviews, and those interviews are conducted by different managers.

We've developed interview tools over the years that help us rank candidates, and that keep our hiring managers from inadvertently asking inappropriate questions. During any given round of hiring, we ask the same questions of all applicants and score the answers. Only the top scorers get second interviews, which saves valuable managerial time.

To be frank, we ask very simple questions. We're not trying to find someone to develop a new strain of antibiotic and secure government grants for the research. We need people who really want to work. We need people who smile often. People who enjoy keeping busy for an entire shift, and who aren't freaked out by seeing long lines of customers every day.

If we can find people who impress upon us they fit this bill, we'll bring them aboard. We also look to our own employees to recommend their friends and family members. We've had as many as four members of a family work for us at the same time, which we really like. It makes for a great work environment. If you have an employee who is an all star and they recommend their brother, why wouldn't you jump at the opportunity? We're a family owned and run place, and it seems like the right thing to do here.

What kinds of marketing do you do, outside of social media?

Not much. We only half-jokingly tell the army of sales people who call on us that our annual advertising and marketing budget is zero.

We really run very few ads, and we really do rely heavily on word of mouth to grow our businesses. The handful of advertisements we do run are usually as a courtesy to an organization or business we really care for. That said, we spend a bunch of money on marketing. We just don't do it in conventional ways.

We have an annual Customer Appreciation Day, when we open our doors and serve as many people as we can for free. We streamline the menu, offer canned sodas instead of fountain drinks to keep things moving along, and have served more than 6,000 free meals during the day of the promotion. Free Days around here usually mean someone is getting a free meal every six seconds we are open. It's a pretty cool thing to watch.

We do this to thank our loyal customers for their patronage, and at the same time attract new customers. The buzz created by this annual event is pretty overwhelming. We've had years when every TV news channel in town picked up the story, as well as radio stations, blogs, and the social media crowd. Obviously feeding 6,000+ people isn't cheap, but we think the investment pays off pretty quickly. It doesn't take many converted first-timers for this approach to pay off.

We are also the "Home of the Free Birthday Meal" offering guests $10 to buy anything they wish on their birthday. Since we also own Joe's Farm Grill and Joe is a partner in Liberty Market across the street from us, we have created the #bdaytrifecta Twitter hashtag to encourage people to go to all three places on their special day.

People generally think we are nuts, especially in encouraging people to eat three meals without paying a dime. But the truth is people don't usually like to eat alone. They will likely spend more than $10, and they rarely celebrate the passing of another year without friends or family. So what happens is we end up seeing a very happy group join us at all three places, and everyone from the happy group shares their story via social media, and among friends.

We think it is probably our most successful marketing tool. People seem to like it too, as we give away over 1,000 free birthday meals every month here at the BBQ.

How important is technology to your restaurant, and what tools help make you run more efficiently?

We love technology. We are all "Mac guys" and love the elegant simplicity seen in Apple's products. We have to balance our desire to employ the latest technology with our need to stay thematically true to our place — a 1940's agriculturally themed restaurant in a town that was once known as the hay capitol of the world.

We have a Mac Mini hidden under a counter powering a display board that was custom built to look like an old TV. The point of sale system is state of the art. We have cameras everywhere, which are monitored via the web. Our employees use Schedulefly from home or their phones. We're moving payroll to the web, which will allow employees to check their timecards online too. The back office has a battery of PCs and Macs set up to allow for engaging in social media, checking sales and product mix, and recording these things so we can use these tools to forecast scheduling and food prep.

We know we will likely employ online or mobile ordering soon. While we personally like being early adopters, getting something in your restaurants because it is new and hip doesn't always make sense. When we do something we want to do it right, and so jumping in and trying to let customers order from phones, iPads or online before we have tested how those orders are worked in to the system doesn't make sense. Instead, we'll continue to let people get catering quotes online, while we continue looking at building apps that might allow more people to order more food more easily!

Highlights – A quick recap of Tad's key points...

- ✓ Unlearn your corporate mindset

- ✓ Build an institution

- ✓ Don't let conventional wisdom rule

- ✓ Give incredible benefits to keep incredible employees

- ✓ Social media can help make personal connections

- ✓ Unconventional marketing can generate huge results

Persistence, design
& never cutting corners

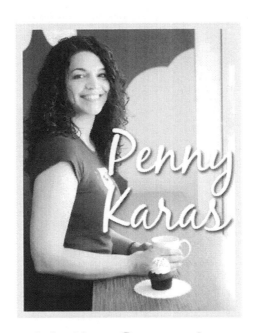

Hello Cupcake
20+ employees
Washington, DC
Restaurant owner since 2008
www.hellocupcakeonline.com

Penny Karas left a career in policy-related communications work in Washington, D.C. to start Hello Cupcake. She opened her first store in 2008, and is getting ready to open a second location soon, as well as launch a national shipping platform. Hello Cupcake makes gourmet cupcakes fresh from scratch, all day, every day, using high-quality, fresh, seasonal ingredients. Penny keeps things simple, leverages really cool design to enhance her brand and refuses to sacrifice the quality of her ingredients. Her passion for her business is contagious

— you start craving cupcakes when you're speaking with her over the phone! She's learned a ton in just a few years, and we're stoked to be able to share some of her philosophies and advice. Enjoy...

How did you get the idea for Hello Cupcake?

I actually grew up in a restaurant. My dad was a chef/owner, and I have always been involved in food. But initially I went in a totally different direction, attending college and grad school to do policy-related communications work in D.C. for many years. But then I decided I wanted to get back into food.

I was always a baker, and my husband encouraged me, so we brainstormed this concept based on things we'd seen in the market. This was in 2004 or so when cupcakes were just starting to surface.

It took me a few years to develop the concept, develop the recipes and get it off the ground with my actual storefront. I did catering out of my home for a while as I was perfecting the recipes and building out the store, and then we opened our store in August of 2008.

And how is it going?

It's going terrifically. We've blown away all of the predictions that we made in our original business plan that we used to get our funding. But I of course had already blown it way out of proportion to get my funding. [Laughs]

We're about to open our second store, and out of that store we're actually going to start doing nationwide shipping. So I couldn't have asked for a better success story for this shop. I'm thrilled with what's happened.

What are the important things to consider when you're baking out a concept and putting together a plan?

Well, these are things that are important to me personally, and they have turned out to be important to the successful operation of my business as well. As a business owner, you really have to live your own philosophy in your business.

First of all, even when I was baking out of my home kitchen, I never cut corners. I did it in small batches, and it was all done from scratch. That continues to be an important element of the business.

We haven't gone to any sort of mixes, even though our suppliers are constantly pushing us to buy their mixes. We do everything from scratch. We juice our own lemons, we crack our own eggs – we don't even use liquid eggs. So it really does have a home baked feel about it.

Another important thing – and another place where my husband comes in – is that the shop has a very high design concept. He's an architect, and he's won five design awards for the shop. The concept of brand experience, where you're in a space that itself is part of the brand – that's really important to me as well.

And the third thing that's important that's been part of our brand from the very beginning is the customer experience. The experience the customers have when they come, when they're there and when they leave. We make sure they walk out with a smile on their face.

Tell me about the plan you used to get funding.

I put together a short-term plan and a longer-term outlook. It was a pretty traditional business plan. I used business planning software to do it. I had never done that before, so I highly recommend getting good business planning software. It guides you through the process and you basically just plug things in.

I counted on a couple of successful business-owner friends to review it for me and to tell me where a bank would call me on things. Then I went to the bank and I knocked on the door, and I wouldn't take no for an answer. I stuck my business plan in front of them, and they said, "Oh no, no, no, no, no. This is ridiculous. Cupcakes? No." And I was like, "Yes! Trust me." [Laughs]

So that's basically what it was. I was very persistent. Every time they asked me for some other piece of information that was a pain in the ass for me to get and to put together, I would do it. I would put it in front of them, and I finally convinced them that this was something that they could support.

At the time it was a little bit easier to get money. Now, the banks are coming to *me* for my second store, which is really a huge turnaround. It's been kind of fun to be able to shop the banks instead of going begging.

You wouldn't take "No" for an answer. What advice do you have for somebody that gets turned down at the bank? Do you go to multiple banks?

Yes. Go to another bank. I was a little bit wary of getting private investors for the business. I'm a little more traditional. I was more comfortable just getting a traditional business loan with a traditional rate of interest, where I didn't have to worry about giving anybody a return on their investment.

So I took my business plan and shopped it around. Every bank laughed at me at the time. But I had a pretty good existing relationship with SunTrust.

I just worked on them. I developed a good relationship there, and we kept talking about options, including whether to do an SBA loan. We finally came to a conclusion about the type of loan that would work, and they agreed to do it.

I'd say from the time I first contacted them until the day we closed took 10 months. That's a long time to be working on that relationship to try to get them to hand over the money.

From what I learned from the process, I tell them to double their imagined budget and their imagined timeline for starting their business. [Laughs]

How important has location been to your success?

It's been key. We are in the city across the street from a very busy metro station. It's key in a number of ways. It's key because it's just a great location – there's lots of people walking around.

It's also key because the area also meshes very well with our brand. We're a very upscale, urban brand, appealing to young professionals, and that's the part of town that we're in. We're right in between the neighborhoods where people live and where they work. We're right at this very busy metro stop. There are lots of other small, independent businesses around us. It's not an area of town that has become national "chainified," like other parts of town.

What is one of your biggest challenges?

Trying to figure out how to manage all of the turnover in this business. I have a core group of people who've been with me from the beginning, and the rest of it is like a revolving door. It's tough to figure out how to make that not be the case. We've got a lot of college students who move on. However, I feel like I can really depend on the core group to help as we move forward.

When did you decide to open a second location and what have you learned from the process?

We're close to opening a second location, and we're going to do nationwide shipping. I had always had it in my mind that we would expand, but I think we're probably not going to expand to more than two stores at this point. I think with the second store and the nationwide shipping, I've pretty much made a decision that shipping from one location opens up a huge market for us, versus trying to open stores in multiple locations.

Why do nationwide shipping versus opening other locations?

It's just a much bigger market, with a much smaller footprint in terms of having to open new shops. As we open new shops, we could have opened a central kitchen somewhere, from which we supply all our shops. And that was one thing we considered doing.

But then, again, a very important part of our brand is that we make this stuff from scratch on site. People walk into the shop and they smell stuff baking. They smell walnuts toasting, or they smell coconut toasting in the oven. We do the prep work. We do the baking. We do the frosting. That's part of the experience of walking into one of our shops, and going to a central location doesn't give you that experience. So we nixed that idea.

But the thought of opening multiple shops with each having its own kitchen was pretty daunting. Opening a second shop means splitting my time between two shops, and really kind of pulling myself out of the day-to-day operation of the shops, and being at more of a corporate level.

Managing a bunch of shops just seemed like a more daunting task than having a facility where we could ship to our market. Now we can keep that home-baked brand and still ship to people in California. They'll get the same cupcakes that were baked the day before.

You mentioned design as well as the smells of the store being important parts of the customer experience. How do you accomplish that with nationwide shipping?

We have developed a packaging system that relies heavily on our visual brand, which is very much a part of the store brand. And it's got that very modern feel and appeal. So customers will experience it through the package that they receive the cupcakes in.

Also, we're going to flash freeze the cupcakes so they will arrive the next day or the day after. They are essentially as fresh as when we pulled them out of the oven. When customers open the box, they will actually get a whiff of them, which is sort of the same as the experience as walking into the shop and smelling the baking cupcakes.

So it was a very intentional parallel between the packaging and the design of our shop.

How will you create awareness nationally?

We'll be doing a number of things. The most important thing that we do now in terms of marketing is media campaigns. We do a lot of public relations, but we don't do much traditional advertising. We do some social media stuff with our Facebook page and we get a lot of news coverage. We've been on national television and NPR [National Public Radio], as well as every newspaper and magazine in town.

That's the approach that we plan to use nationwide as well. I have a terrific PR agency that does that for me. We've developed a nationwide relationship with Kitchen Aid, which sponsored a cupcake design competition that we had in our shop. Kitchen Aid wants to continue doing that as we expand and start shipping nationwide, as we have an obviously similar target market.

The failure rate in your industry is so high. So many people try to do what you've done successfully and they fail. What are people missing?

Honestly, I'm not any kind of expert on my industry. I just have a concept that I think is good, that hit the market at the right time, and is well located for our target market.

I don't know what those other folks are doing wrong because I don't have any insight into their businesses.

I can tell you what I think we've done right. Maybe it's just a mix of what we put together: a great product, a great brand and quite a bit of luck as well.

Are you familiar with Zappos?

What self-respecting woman isn't? [Laughs]

You remind me a bit of what Zappos does, providing a great customer experience that entices people to shop more.

Well, they're not the cheapest, so people are not shopping there for discount shopping. It is all about the experience.

Highlights – A quick recap of Penny's key points...

✓ Find trusted advisors to poke holes in your business plan

✓ Never cut corners

✓ Don't take no for an answer at the bank

✓ Double your projected budget and time frame to get started

✓ Marry your location with your brand

Delegation, the little things
& checking your ego at the door

Glowbal Group
800+ employees
Vancouver, BC
Restaurant owner since 1996
www.glowbalgroup.com

After many years as an executive chef at some of Canada's most famous five-star restaurants, Emad has owned successful restaurants in Toronto and Vancouver for more than 15 years. He started Glowbal Group in 2002, and has been opening a restaurant almost every year since. His restaurants (Italian Kitchen, Coast, Sanafir, Trattoria, glowbal grill, Society) are perennially among the most popular, successful restaurants in Vancouver. The energy, bustle and allure of these celebrated Vancouver restaurants are what most people notice first. But it goes far beyond just flash and excitement. These are serious culinary hotspots. I spent 30 minutes talking to Emad. I could have talked to him all day...

How did you get started in the restaurant business?

In 1984 I came to Canada. I was working on my accounting degree, and I was looking for a job. I walked into a Hilton Hotel, and for my luck, the executive chef at The Hilton, Albert Schnell, was one of the top chefs in the world. I got a job as a kitchen helper, and I worked with him for a little bit, and he saw some very hard work and talent, so I moved up the ranks quite fast.

I was the youngest executive chef in Toronto by the age of 25, running a superstar restaurant in Toronto called Aqua. I was the executive chef there until '94. I was the executive chef at one other boutique restaurant outside of Toronto, then I went to Vancouver to be the chef of a restaurant called Joportes, which was at that time the number one restaurant in sales in British Columbia.

So during my career I did work with some great chefs, and it gave me great experience as a chef. Business sense hadn't really hit me yet. I had little spurts of it, partly because my accounting degree made me understand numbers very well. So I was the only executive chef that could talk to the owners about numbers. I was quite successful making huge profits for my owners. Chefs are not known for that.

When I went on my own and started opening my own restaurants, it became a very easy transition. I started with a small café in Toronto, and it worked well. I opened a restaurant next door – a small little fine-dining place. It also worked very well. I sold them both and I opened something bigger in Vancouver nine years ago, and started

Glowbal. We're averaging a new business each year. We have six restaurants, two lounges, a catering division and a bar.

The growth of the company has gone very well. We have 800 employees now.

Take me back to your first restaurant in Toronto. What made it work?

That was a very simple café. I didn't have any money in my pocket. I learned one thing about working in five-star restaurants: how to become a great chef. But how can you be humble to just run a café, and not lose the passion in your heart? That's very important.

People get so wrapped up with the business that they do, that they forget that they are only in the business to make money. That café was $85,000 when we bought it, and we only gave them a $40,000 deposit. I broke into my retirement plan, and took a hit on it in taxes. I borrowed cash from my brother, and he and my cousin came in with me as partners.

We just wanted to get our feet wet, so first we just had some sandwiches and some pastas. Then the place was becoming quite busy, because I brought in the five-star philosophy of using fresh food, but I made it very affordable, and very simple, and a very "mama and papa" place.

I think that's when I got it in my head to come away from that big fine-dining philosophy, and how I can create a comfortable feeling in my businesses. So it taught me a lot, running a little bistro where you could walk in and have a grilled chicken sandwich, or just a little fresh pasta, but it was a very high-quality pasta or sandwich, and it was done very cheap.

We were very happy, because we had money in our pocket. We didn't care too much to run the numbers – on whether we were running 28% food costs, and stuff like that. We just focused on making people happy, and the money would come after that. That had a big impact on my philosophy in the restaurant business. As much as we know the numbers, we don't take shortcuts when it comes to our customers. The customer will always get high-quality items for a very good price.

I will guarantee in our city that if the restaurant next door has the same steak on the menu, it's going to cost a little bit more than mine. We've found how to save money other ways than saving it on the plate, like saving it on the labor that's going to serve the plate.

How do you do that?

Well, Schedulefly helps us a lot. The managers can – in an instant – contact 100 waiters via text message and tell them something based on how the tables are turning. So we could ask them to come in a half an hour later if we're slow. Well, that half an hour that's saved – the customer doesn't see it because there's nobody in the restaurant, so it helps us control our labor costs.

The way it's done in Canada is different than in the states because our labor costs are much higher. When you pay $8 an hour – or $10 in Ontario – and they make tips, and you don't charge $40 for a tenderloin, how can you make money? You do it by saving 15 minutes or 30 minutes on labor. You don't bring your whole team at 11:30 for a 12:00 opening. If you have 40 waiters on the floor, you bring 15 at 11:30, and 15 at 11:45, and 10 at 12:00. And suddenly that half an hour and that 15 minutes per person that you saved adds up to big numbers here. We might save 400 hours a month that way. So this is understanding how to give the customer the good service and the good food, without affecting the environment the customer is in.

We also see savings by training our managers to understand numbers on everything. We have a financial meeting with our managers every month, and we go through all the little details, like how much paper has been used. I mean, we're a small company, but we still run it like a Fortune 500. So how can we save on things like when to light the candle on the table? Do you light it at 5:00 in the summer time, or light it at 7:00 when the daylight is gone? Well that two hour difference will save you $400 or $500 per month in fuel.

You employee 800 people. How do you find the right people that will share your passion for serving the customers?

It is difficult, but it starts from the top. We hear all of the time from people, "Oh, I don't know how you get your staff to be that good, or that smiley, or that perfect."

Well, it all starts from the top. If the managers have the same excitement and the same passion that I have, it will flow to the supervisor. And if the supervisor has the same passion and excitement, it's going to flow to the senior waiter. And the senior waiters give it to the waiters.

We're also a very vocal group. Off the cuff. We love having fun at work. At the end of the day, I tell my staff, "Just have fun first." Fun will make everything else great. If you're having fun at work, and you're looking after the customer with the same philosophy, the customer is going to feel it.

We also have service training programs that everybody goes through. We have food and wine tastings every week at all of the restaurants. We have meetings every week about how to develop the menus better, and how to create different concepts and make the concepts feel better.

We have discussions with the chefs about how to open their eyes because the chefs are all wearing blinders. We open some of their eyes very well. For instance, I just lost one of my best executive chefs in the company because he decided to open a food cart on the street. He realized that it's not about your ego, it's about the business sense. He's trying to do the same sort of steps that we did, so he decided he wanted to start his business by opening a gourmet food cart selling organic sandwiches.

I was very happy for him, because it showed that what we tried to do works. We want everybody to be successful. I really would not be upset if he left me to open across the street and become my competition because it would make me stronger.

What have you learned about partnerships?

I have great partners with me. I think the success of the company is because I am very close to my partners. It is very difficult to break through us. If your partners know that you are very fair with them – they're going to respect you, and they're going to be giving more to you than you're giving them.

My partners know that sometimes when a month is not doing very well, that I sacrifice some of my percentage for that month. They know that I don't have to because there are lots of fat months to cover it, but at the end of the day I'm making very good money, and it's not about the extra $5,000 or $10,000. It's about everybody making good money around me. That makes your partners very, very loyal to you.

How has your role changed as your group has grown?

It's made me change as a person. In the old days, I needed to control everything. Everything had to be in front of my plate. Everything I had to put my finger on.

Then I realized I physically can't be in but so many locations at the same time. So it taught me to be a lot more open in terms of giving. I give my partners lots of leeway to run things. And when they call me sometimes and ask for my opinion, I say, "This is your department. I trust you." By letting go like this, it gives me more time to grow as a person. And if I'm growing as a person, everybody around me is going to grow with me.

Why do so many restaurants fail?

I always say, "Let's take the egos out of it. At the end of the day, it's a business." If you approach it through your ego, you'll fail. When I interview people, I tell them, "Let's say I was going to build you a restaurant. It's going to be 40 seats, and you are going to be cooking for superstars, princesses, and kings. Your name is going to be one of the best chefs in the city. With 40 seats, you'll be working six, seven days a week because you'll be the only one that can do it. Or, we could open a fish and chips stand, and the line will be around the block seven days a week, and it will be very profitable, and you won't have to be there much. Which are you going to own?"

It's funny how the people who pick the first one took the business sense out of it. We don't hire them. We're in the business to make money. It's not about egos.

What else causes failures?

You have to know what your clientele wants. You have to know how to produce it, and you have to know how to deliver it to them.

I was reading a book about entrepreneurs, and about a very big chef in New York. A customer told the server the restaurant should have fried calamari on the menu, and he told the chef. The chef said, "I'm not going to put fried calamari on the menu." A week later another customer suggested they should put fried calamari on the menu. So the server told the chef, and the chef decided to put the dish on the menu, but he called it something like "Squid with drizzled oil," or something similar. It made it sound confusing, and nobody ordered it.

The truth is, we're in the business to serve people walking through the door. If the customer wants fried calamari, we'll get them fried calamari. What the customer wants, the customer gets, and that's why people keep coming back.

At the end of the day, it has to be a business decision. Decisions need to be made with emotions taken out of them. We do things based on what the customer wants to eat, not what our egos tell us to do.

Highlights – A quick recap of Emad's key points...

✓ Little details, like when you light your candles, are very important

✓ Wish for your teammates' success, even if it means losing them

✓ Go above and beyond for your partners

✓ Learn to let go if you want to grow

✓ Take your ego out of the equation

Running lean, working to live
& feeding customers like they're friends

Beau Jo's
300+ employees
Denver, CO
Restaurant owner since 1973
www.beaujos.com

Chip Bair has been at it for 37 years. When he bought a tiny little pizza place on a side street in Idaho Springs, CO, $30 was a big day. He did everything from sleeping on the restaurant floor, to recycling the paper from the printing business behind Beau Jo's to earn gas money to fuel up his car for trips to buy supplies. All of the sacrifices paid off because Beau Jo's is now legendary among Colorado outdoor enthusiasts. Chip is as cool as the other side of the pillow, and the kind of guy who would give you the shirt off of his back. He makes awesome pizzas, has happy employees and customers and has *learned more than a few lessons over the years. Here's what he had to say...*

How did you get started?

I purchased Beau Jo's on April 1st, 1973. I bought it from a couple named Beau and Joanne, hence the name. So I just told you what is an obvious lie on our menu, because we go into this story about pizza pie and the wooly mammoth, which isn't really true.

Beau and Joanne opened it in Idaho Springs, CO, a small mining town of 1,800 people on Interstate 70, about 20 miles west of Denver. They were off on a side street, and they sat somewhere between 15 and 18 people. The kitchen was comprised mostly of old tables from a domestic kitchen. Two or three domestic refrigerators. We had a small deck pizza oven, and a small mixer. That was pretty much the equipment side of it. Thirty dollars back then was a big day when I first took it over.

They had one part-time girl named Patsy-Mae. She taught me what to do and how to do things. We made the sauce and the dough daily. They used dehydrated onions, canned mushrooms and dehydrated green peppers. I remember opening a five-pound tin of the onions, and it was just dry flakes, and you'd have to throw water in it and let them hydrate over night.

What changes did you make?

I started out with the concept of doing everything from scratch and fresh. The first thing I did was to get rid of the dehydrated onions, green peppers and mushrooms, and use all fresh stuff. The second thing I did was to add whole wheat crust to our menu.

I had gotten a little hand coffee grinder, and I'd get Colombian coffee beans, and I'd sit there when things were slow – which was a lot of the time – and I'd grind my coffee by myself by hand. So that was the kind of stuff that we were trying to do, and I've continued doing those types of things to this day.

We always try to look forward, and I've always tried to do a healthier product. At the very beginning, we took the sugar out of the dough recipe and the sauce and started using honey instead.

What got you interested in buying a pizza business?

One of our family's friends was president of Gino's, a large frozen food manufacturer. Our families would get together on occasion. They had two daughters, and I had two sisters, so when we'd get together, the girls would go off and play, and I would sit with my father and Mr. Workman, and listen to them talk about business. I found that very entertaining.

I had been selling shoes, but when the opportunity arose for me to move in to the mountains – which I had definitely been wanting to do – and get into business for myself, I took it. I paid $6,500 to buy the restaurant. The contract was for $8,000, but if I made my payments on time I ended up getting a $1,500 discount, so that was a good opportunity.

I started out and my rent factor was about $100 per month. We had 760 square feet, which included a little tiny shower in the restaurant. At first I slept on the floor of the restaurant for a couple of months or so. Then I finally got a little cabin that I got on a trade with the dog catcher for $25 of pizza per month, which worked out real good for me.

That's awesome. You did what you had to do. What happened from there?

I remember driving around with Beau when he was training me, and taking me down to meet the purveyors, and he said he would occasionally close up and go camping for two or three days. Initially, I thought that schedule would be fun, but then I realized people have to eat seven days a week, and if they come over, and you're not open, they're probably not going to come back soon. So after the first week, I started staying open seven days a week, and I kept consistent hours.

What was the most important issue on your mind at the time?

At that point, I had absolutely no concept of food costs. In '73 we had 20% interest rates, and inflation was really running rampant. My costs were going up all of the time, so I'd have to be raising prices on the pizzas. But I figured if I was raising prices, then I'd have to put more stuff on them.

Like I said, I didn't have any concept of food costs. I would still go down and visit friends in Denver, so I'd always bring pizzas with me. So as I loaded up the pizzas for Denver, I thought, "We're not going to skimp on our ingredients for our friends. We're not going to skimp on anything. We're going to get the best and the most ingredients. At Beau Jo's we'll always make the pizzas like we were making them for our friends." That was kind of how we developed the pizza.

I suppose your changes worked?

They seemed to. After about nine months over on the side street in Idaho Springs, we had started getting pretty busy, and the 18 seats weren't really working any more. The three refrigerators that we had for our inventory didn't cut it. That cabin I was renting had two rooms, one of which was full of flour, cans of tomato sauce, and black olives, and things like that.

I negotiated to move out onto Main Street to a place with 40 seats and a walk-in cooler, which was amazing! We never thought we'd fill up that walk-in, but things just kind of kept on growing. That location now seats 600. We've grown, remodeled, and expanded that location over the years somewhere around 25 times. We are now in four buildings.

Tell me about your first expansion to a new location.

The first time we expanded out of Idaho Springs was 1975. I'm a double Gemini, and I have this tendency to do things in twos for some reason, so we opened up a licensed unit in Denver in October of '75, and two weeks later I opened up another store in Crested Butte, CO. Went from one to three. Not a good idea. Don't recommend it. I highly recommend doing that type of thing, but not so quickly.

You expanded too quickly?

Yes. I didn't know what I was doing. Running one unit, and being there all of the time yourself is one thing, but going to two units is a totally different dynamic. I went from one to three in two weeks, and that was not a good thing.

Crested Butte, home of a popular ski mountain, was a six hour drive. I was doing that three times a week. At the time I was already working 18 to 20 hours a day anyway, so putting a six hour drive – one way – three times a week on top of that was really difficult.

I didn't have management systems at that point in time. I didn't have good cost controls, training or any of the stuff you need to expand.

You had a partner in Crested Butte, right?

Yes. He owned the movie theater there. He was supposed to put like $5,000 into the restaurant, and he never did.

We got the world's fastest liquor license up there. From start to finish, we got our license in 10 days. Just amazing. We went in there and did a little remodeling, and cleaned it up. We opened up before Thanksgiving, and the mountain didn't even open up until after Thanksgiving that year. '75 was a real bad year for snow, and it was before they made snow out there.

So they weren't getting any snow, and there was nobody in town, and business was really slow. This partner I had, that didn't put any money into it — but the liquor license happened to have been in his name — was not happy with the fact that there wasn't any business, even though there wasn't any business in town.

He got upset about it one day, and wound up having a meeting with the sheriff and the mayor to try to figure out how to close us down. Because the liquor license was in his name, he finally came in and just took the liquor license off of the wall. Then we didn't have a liquor license, so we couldn't sell liquor. That was pretty much the end of that business. So choose your partners well, if you're going to have partners. Partners are really tough.

What about the other store you opened in Denver at the same time?

That was a partnership that a couple of guys had put together, and they weren't doing well. They had a couple of managers who were going out and taking people to dinner at all kinds of places around town, and just spending all kinds of money. They had no controls whatsoever.

I ended up going in and taking over, and got it turned around. At that point I was down to two locations, but I came pretty close to losing pretty much the whole ball of wax because of expanding too quickly without having the knowledge and the background, and not knowing what the heck I was doing. I had a wonderful product, but I didn't have a partner and I didn't have anybody that I could really trust to help me do it. And you can't do it all by yourself.

We had a basement in that Denver location, and we set up our office down there. It was small and a little depressing, but it kept costs down, and making every penny count was real important. It still is. It always has been.

I guess so, since you slept on the floor when you first started! What are some other ways you made every penny count early on?

When I was first getting started I drove a Lotus Europa, which was a very small sports car. It wasn't very good for supply runs. In the days before suppliers would deliver to us up here in the mountains, I would pull up with my Lotus, and I would have things stuck every which way in that vehicle. Finally, after a month or two of that, I finally bought myself a '56 Ford pickup.

To cover the cost of gas, I would load up my truck with the waste overruns of the newspaper print company next door, and take it down and recycle it. I'd make $6 or $10 for gas to go pick up my supplies and drive back up. Again, I was saving every penny that I could and doing everything I could to make it profitable. That was just one more little thing that I was able to do.

What else were you learning at this point?

That you've always got to know where you're at. You've gotta have good books and good accounting. You've got to have good mentors. I had a couple of great individuals for many years. I had a board of directors for a number of years.

One gentleman on my board had been a vice president for Mr. Steak. Another gentleman on my board was a real estate broker. Between the two of them they were really wonderful at negotiating leases. That was one of our early strengths, was our leases.

Do you still run a lean business?

You have to. Probably most businesses are like this, but in the restaurant business, definitely. It's a penny business. You've gotta watch those pennies because those pennies add up to dollars. And they add up to dollars pretty quickly.

What else have you learned?

Things don't stay the same. You either go forward or you go backward. We constantly have to be thinking about how to do a better job.

You also need to be aware of what your talents are. What you do well, and what you don't do well. I'm not a real detailed person. I'm more conceptual. So I've tried to bring people in that were more detailed to run the company – the day-to-day operations.

You've always been moving forward?

There was one point in time where we quit innovating. We were way far ahead of where everybody else was. Again, we had started doing whole wheat pizza in 1973, and as far as I know we were the first ones in the country that did it. We had an international collection of pizzas in 1975, where we had different sauces, and different cheeses. I mean I guess my philosophy had always been that with a pizza, you have a platform of some bread – which can be any kind of bread – and you can put anything on it. That was kind of how pizza started back in Italy. It was a peasant food, and they would just put whatever on it, and we did that.

But we sat back for a while, and we started to lose our edge. We had people in there running the day-to-day operations for a time that were probably more focused on the bottom line than putting out the best product, and we lost some quality for a while.

I took back control of operations after a while, and we had to almost reinvent ourselves. We went back to some of the basic things that we had been doing in the past, which had gotten lost because of looking at the bottom line. Looking at that bottom line a little too closely, and forgetting about who you are, can really hurt you.

Fortunately we discovered it and were able to fix it, but quality had declined for a while. That's not a good thing. You can't maintain business that way.

How do you find the people that give your guests the kind of experience you want to give them?

People are probably the biggest asset you have. You have the concept, and then your people come directly thereafter, or parallel, or whatever.

I guess I'm kind of a hippy from the '60s or '70s, and I've always tried to look at things with a rosy outlook and tried to do what's right by the company and its employees. We have some waitresses whose mothers had worked for me. Most of our managers have been with us for 12 to 15 years. The store that opened in South Dakota was opened by a manager that started working for us in the mid '80s. She and her husband decided they wanted to move up to Rapid City, and she wanted to continue with our business. So we helped set her up, and she's really happy up there and doing a really good job with it. She'd been with us for a really long time, and knew what we were doing and what we were about.

I understand you provide a lot of good employee benefits.

We do things for our employees such as having paid vacations, even for our dishwashers. We have annual ski passes that are available for our staff to use. We have good health insurance for our management staff. We used to pay all of it for the whole family, up until the last several years. We still try to do the vast majority of it, but that gets harder and harder all of the time.

The restaurant industry tends to beat management staff up a lot. Typically in chain restaurants, managers will work 60 to 80 hours per week. Our managers work typically 40 to 45 hours per week. We might not pay them what they could make at restaurants where they'd work 80 hours per week, but we've always felt that there needs to be a balance between working and your life. So we've always had our managers working a 45 hour week, and that's one reason why we retain them.

We deal with them as humans and equals, and look for input. I've seen people go in and berate their employees, and that's just not the way we are. We believe in the family and the strength of it. We try to follow through with that with the things that we do for our employees.

We pay our employees weekly. Most people pay every other week or whatever. We pay weekly, and that makes it a little bit easier for them. We have a good liberal meal policy, and we try to have a good positive work environment for people.

So you have plans to franchise Beau Jo's?

We have talked about if for years, and I think we are at that point in time where we're finally going to do it. I've always kind of backed off of franchising because it's a different business. I've been in the restaurant business for years and years. With a franchise, I have a different customer. As a franchise organization, your customer is now the franchisee, instead of the person that's eating the pizza.

So there are some things that we're going to have to do. Over the years we've been putting training programs together, and accounting programs, and things like that. We've always gotten requests for franchising, and it's time to do it.

Do you have any specific goals?

We're putting together a group of people to run the company and develop the franchising program. So that's just now being put together and we don't have any details as far as goals. At this point in time I'm saying 100 restaurants in the next 10 years. We might find that we can do that a whole lot quicker, but I don't want to expand too fast.

Highlights – A quick recap of Chip's key points...

✓ Be willing to sleep on the floor

✓ People eat with their eyes

✓ Always run lean

✓ Feed your customers like you'd feed your friends

✓ Find others to fill your gaps

✓ Watch the bottom line, but not with tunnel vision

Simple fundamentals, buying buildings & using your marketing budget on comps

Emmit's Irish Pub & Eatery
30+ employees
Chicago, IL
Restaurant owner since 1996
www.emmits.com

Kevin was a Chicago fireman when he helped start Emmit's Irish Pub & Eatery, and he's still a fireman today. Meanwhile, he and his partner, Ron Halvorsen (a retired Chicago fireman), have turned Emmit's into a popular and successful neighborhood pub – popular enough that movie and television bar scenes are routinely shot there ("Uncle Buck," "Only the Lonely," "Blink," "Backdraft," "Ocean's Eleven," "Ocean's Twelve," and many more). Kevin is a great guy – nice, easy to talk to, fair, selfless and hard working. The coolest part about Kevin's story was hearing him talk about keeping things simple, having a clear focus on how important his staff is and not being afraid to work really hard. When you speak to Kevin, he makes the challenging job of running a successful restaurant seem simple...

How did you get involved in owning a restaurant?

My partner, Ron Halvorsen, and I are firemen. We worked together and were friends, and Ron was a builder on the side. Seventeen years or so ago, he wanted to establish some type of a bar, so he found the building that we're in now, which was initially a bank back in the '20s. It was the Italian Savings & Trust, and it had been for sale for nearly six years.

It took us about two and a half years to gut and rehab a beautiful old building. We opened the doors in '96 as a neighborhood Irish pub. When we opened the doors, Ronnie was pretty much running it with a manager, and then I got actively involved in it, and here we are 17 years later.

How much did you know about running restaurants before you opened?

We went into it with very little experience. The only experience Ronnie had in the restaurant was being a waiter at IHOP when he was in high school. It was trial by fire. We were both willing to jump in without a net and work real hard, and that's pretty much it. We learned as we went.

What did you focus on?

Our fundamentals were real simple: be a neighborhood pub in an area that's quickly becoming a neighborhood. It wasn't much of a neighborhood then, but it's real close to downtown, and not too many places downtown would buy a regular a drink. We wanted to change that.

We hired a staff that took ownership. We told them to run it as if it's their own. We of course monitor everything pretty closely, but we give them the freedom to operate as if it were their own. It's a very non-corporate type of atmosphere. Because of that, we've got staff that's been here since we opened.

We try to maintain that level of service to the people in the neighborhood that come in. We have lots of regulars. We try to instill in the staff to know what they drink, to know their names, to welcome them when they walk in the door, and just don't take any of that for granted.

And then just through determination and hard work, and learning from a lot of mistakes that we made, we just keep moving forward. Fortunately we've been fairly successful. The recession has hurt us a little bit, but we operate lean enough where we're able to manage.

What did you learn in the first few years that you had not thought of coming into it?

The hours, were tough, but we were in for a penny, in for a pound. We had so much money invested in it initially that, believe me, if I could have sold it for my investment after that second year and get out, I probably would have. Thank God I didn't do that, because it's proven to be successful.

242

So you had a few really good core philosophies going into it?

Not real good ones. Just basic, like treating people how you like to be treated.

I got married a little later, so I went out to a lot of bars, restaurants, clubs, etc. Certain ones treated you right, and certain ones could care less whether you came back. So it's little simple things we notice that seemed to make the difference, and we tried to instill that. It's easier said than done.

I think a lot of it's just the luck of the employees that you hire. You try to get good ones, and you really don't know how good they are until after they work here a few months. We've been fortunate in that respect. At least, we like to think so.

In the early years, when things were slow, we might book a big party, and we'd always say we've got shamrocks on our asses, because it always seemed to just work out.

Once we got over that initial hurdle and paid off the loans, the economy was picking up, and things seemed to really take off. Then we were just fortunate to have a building that a lot of the studios were familiar with, so we got a lot of free publicity through different movies, television commercials and things like that that we didn't have to pay for.

We've never spent a lot of money in marketing. I always thought that instead of marketing to the unknown, we'd spend that money and market it to the people that were coming in. And how we do that is, we comp a lot of drinks for people. If they have a certain amount, or if there's a celebration, we comp it, and we make sure it's on their tab so they can see that they're being comped.

I don't know where you grew up, but did you ever go into a neighborhood bar after a softball game, and after three or four beers, the neighborhood bar would buy you one? Well it seems like a lot of establishments, especially downtown, got away from that. So we try to incorporate that into our philosophy.

Does that lead to you having a lot of repeat customers?

Yes, and that's what keeps us going. Throughout the years, people have gotten married and moved on. But the common denominator, if people have friends in from out of town, they'll come in and say, "This is my bar." And that feels good. You know you're doing something right if they're bringing guests from out of town here.

Many restaurant partnerships fail. What goes into making a partnership successful?

Partnerships are extremely tough. I know because I've got other partnerships with real estate deals. First and foremost, there's got to be an unbelievable trust between the two partners.

Also, you've got to be opposites. I think opposites attract. There are certain aspects that some are going to be better at than others. Ronnie is kind of a larger-than-life character, and he's very social. Meanwhile, I'm more the bookkeeper. I'm social enough, but I don't need to be up and meeting and greeting. I'd rather come in in the morning, get the books done, get the orders in, and then get out of here by six o'clock.

Ronnie is the opposite. Ronnie will be sitting up at the corner of the bar greeting people as they come in the door. If there's a celebration, he'll be buying a round of shots. He's pretty much the face of the place, and I'm kind of the guy behind the scenes. And that's worked out.

The failure rate in your industry is extraordinarily high. You two were firemen. Conventional wisdom would have probably been that you wouldn't have made it. But you did. What keeps other people from doing what you did?

I think the number one reason is not being willing to put in the hard work. It takes long hours and complete dedication. There are lot of times – we've found it ourselves – where you think it's not gonna work, but you've just gotta persevere. I mean we're crazy enough to have just bought another building right now.

Location is also extremely important. We're in a good location. When we first opened here, there wasn't a lot of competition. We're not too far from the United Center, where the Bulls and the Blackhawks play. When we opened in '96, we got huge crowds before and after the games. Well, in the interim, between '96 and now with the real estate boom, and consequent bust, they redeveloped all of the area around United Center. So now there are probably 40 new bars between there and here that weren't here in '96. So we have to work harder to draw that crowd in.

The atmosphere is important too. We've got a unique building. It's on a corner and is pie-shaped. We've got 15-foot ceilings as soon as you walk in. When people walk in and they're from out of town, they say, "This looks like what I would expect a Chicago bar to look like." So right there, when you walk in the door and you're greeted, the atmosphere is crucial.

Of course, if you're not providing good service or good food, that's not going to work. And you've also got the price formula. Downtown prices – everything a few blocks away – are a little bit higher. If you go to the northwest side, they're considerably cheaper. We try to balance on that edge where we're not lowering our prices to the point more than we have to. But yet, we're going to pour a fair drink for the price, so people know they're getting their money's worth.

Do you have to revisit your pricing frequently?

You do, because prices are constantly changing, and right now they're all going up. Whether it be the taxes or the price of liquor. It's a balancing act.

I don't want to raise the prices more than I have to, because that can shun people away. Yet I don't want to put specials out there. A lot of places are doing these specials all of the time, and I don't know if that necessarily works. I don't want the customers to get so used to these low-cost specials that when they get charged a regular price, they feel like they're getting short changed.

So what I'll do is maybe bring a different product in, and put it at a lower price. With this economy, there are more and more people calling up now and asking what our specials are, and some of our specials aren't going to compete with what they've got going elsewhere. So we are looking at some other products that are price competitive.

There's a brewery near here in Wisconsin, which is a retro brewery, that we're bringing in next week, called Pabst Blue Ribbon. They've got a real low price point. So we're going to try it. We're going to try and fit that niche when people call in, and say, "We've got a low price on Pabst Blue Ribbon, one draft, and then a food special." Without really giving the whole house away. And if that's what they're looking for, we'll see if it works.

It's a juggling act. A lot of times in this business, the best laid plans don't always work out. But if you have your finger on the pulse, you can change quickly.

How do you keep your finger on the pulse?

When we initially opened, we didn't have the technology that we have now. Probably 10 to 12 years ago, we got a POS system, which really gives you spot-on numbers, as far as what you sold the day before, what your costs are for items sold. You can look at it on a day-to-day basis, week-to-week, month-to-month, and see where your trends are, and see the products that are moving.

When we first opened in '96, there was a big emphasis on microbrews. Then I saw that kind of wane. A lot of the micro brews went out of business. Then it went more toward the imports. We featured a lot of imports on draft. Now it's come full circle again, and the craft brews are making a big impact again.

We go to the distributors' seminars, and see the products they're bringing in. And a lot of it is just based on sales. I try to do what the customers want. What the customers want is basically what drives our decision, not so much what the best deal is.

You recently bought a new building. What does the future hold?

We've done well enough over the last few years that we were able to stockpile some money and buy a building. It's kind of the same thing that drew me into this place. I really did not want to open another bar or restaurant, per se. And if I did, there are some locations southwest of here which are kind of up and coming artistic areas.

But this is a unique opportunity where this building is. It's got a very nice curb appeal to it. It's in the northwest corner of the city in an area that has been dry for many years, but was just voted wet. So there's really no other bars in this particular area, which is probably middle to upper middle class. People can walk to it and not worry about drinking and driving. People can bring their family and have a burger and a beer, or so forth.

So we're looking to expand there. And again, it's all about the real estate. I've had other firemen that say, "I'm thinking about opening up a bar." I always tell them, "If you can't afford to buy the real estate, or the property, along with the build out and opening your business, I don't think it's worth it."

There are some good and famous restaurants in Chicago that are closing and looking for new locations. I talked to one of their financial guys, and he said, "15 years ago, we negotiated a great lease. However, 15 years later, our lease is up, and now the landlord is really whacking us."

So I look at it from the standpoint of a real estate investment. I know that's crazy now, because real estate's in the tank. But I look at the property first, and then the business second. That's what we did here. And that's what we're going to do over there.

Do you have any concerns about transitioning from one location to two?

Absolutely. But it's like anything else. There are a lot of unknowns, but you can't let the concerns you have immobilize you.

You've been successful at what you're doing, and you're ready for another challenge?

Yes, and it's easy to get complacent. We've been on easy street. We've had this place running like such a clock, that you almost take it for granted. By opening the other place, it gets your juices flowing again, so to speak. The fear. The excitement. The anticipation. The difficulties.

You said you run a lean operation. How do you do that?

You have to keep an eye on payroll and staffing. It's very difficult at times managing the people where you don't overstaff, where you're spending too much money, versus understaffing, where your customers are shortchanged.

We just deal with it. Again, there's no answer for that. We try to staff when we anticipate that we'll have a big crowd, and get them in here. Sometimes we get lambasted when we're understaffed.

What other advice do you have for somebody that's considering opening a restaurant?

I would find out what their family life is like. If they're married. If they're dating. If they plan on getting married shortly. You better make sure your significant other is fully on board.

I was dating when we opened this place, so for a while there, I wasn't married. I don't think I would have been able to do it if I was married, because it consumes all of your time. So I was fortunate.

Now, I've got the knowledge and the time management where I don't feel I have to be there constantly. I don't have the learning curve that I had when we opened initially. When we initially opened, we were open for lunch. I'd get in here at 11:00 am and get out of here at 2:00 am. I certainly wouldn't do that now, with a family.

You almost have to be there all of the time in the initial startup stages. If you don't have your finger on the pulse, no one's gonna operate your business the same way you would. When you walk in the door, you're going to see different things that they don't see. Whether it's a light that's burnt out or a chair that is not aligned properly. When it's your own business, you just pick up on that, and no one else is going to. I don't care how good your manager is.

It's the same as how you always think your kids are always cuter than somebody else's. That's just one of those things. You look at someone else's baby, and yeah, it's cute. But your own baby seems a little cuter. You take that same ownership of your restaurant.

Highlights – A quick recap of Kevin's key points...

- ✓ Keep your fundamentals simple

- ✓ Use your marketing budget on comps

- ✓ Got a family? Think before you leap

- ✓ Pricing is a constant balancing act

- ✓ Buy your building

Growth, innovation
& having "green" DNA

Pi Pizzeria

300+ employees
St. Louis, MO & Washington, D.C.
Restaurant owner since 2008
www.restaurantpi.com

Pi Pizzeria has been wildly successful in a short amount of time. Chris and his partner, Frank Uible, opened their first location on "Pi Day" March 14 (3.14) 2008, and by that October then-Senator and presidential candidate Barack Obama enjoyed some of their pizza after a St. Louis campaign rally. He loved it, and Pi, which was already very popular, became a sensation. They now have four locations and a mobile pizza truck, and they are opening in Washington, D.C. in 2011. Chris left Salesforce.com to open Pi, after buying a recipe for an insanely good deep dish pizza from a small pizzeria that he frequented in San Francisco. He is extremely smart, has great business instincts and has learned quite a bit in the last few years...

You were at Salesforce.com in San Francisco a few years ago, and now you own a highly successful group of restaurants in St. Louis. What happened?

I put myself through high school and college working in the restaurant business. Then I went out to Silicon Valley and was in high tech and finance, and spent the last seven years of my career working at Salesforce.com. I ended up in the sales world there, so I was doing a lot of dining but not working in the business.

I fell in love with this deep dish pizza around the corner from my condo in San Francisco. Serendipitously, the owner bought the condo across the hall from mine, and I just listened to how people talked about this pizza from this small independent pizzeria called Little Star Pizza. I listened to the way that people waxed poetic about it and thought about the fact that San Francisco is kind of a melting pot. People there are from all corners of the country and the globe, and if they were all enjoying it then I thought that perhaps this product was pretty special and had some potential outside of San Francisco.

For a small amount of money, I convinced the owner to sell me the recipe for their deep dish corn meal crust. Then I convinced my best friend in St. Louis to leave his career in the apparel business, and I moved back to St. Louis and opened Pi on Pi Day (3.14) 2008. I stayed with Salesforce.com until about a year ago.

When I left we had just opened our second store, and now we have just opened our fourth, as well as a pizza truck – our mobile unit – and I am now full time in the pizza business. So I took kind of an odd path to being a restaurateur, but it was more about a business opportunity and taking a risk, and thankfully it paid off.

I benefitted from good timing with the market and the economy and pizza being a nice alternative to finer dining. Opening a pizza place in 2008 was much more destined for success than opening something fine dining.

So timing was fortunate, and then in early 2009 getting an endorsement from a guy living at 1600 Pennsylvania Avenue hasn't hurt. I know you can't buy that kind of publicity, so that put us on a much steeper trajectory and allowed us to expand. And thankfully, at two years and change in, we're at four stores and growing.

We don't have any debt, so that helps. It allows us to make decisions to do things aggressively, and not be hindered by bank loans and things that might otherwise hinder your growth.

How did you balance owning a restaurant and still working at Salesforce.com?

There wasn't a lot of balance — just a lot of long days and nights. [Laughs] They knew what I was doing, and they were very patient. I had put in a lot of time and effort into my first few years there, so I was able to do my job with probably not as much effort as I would have liked, but they were excited for me at the same time, and I really owe them a lot. I learned a lot from them, and the CEO, Marc Benioff, who was definitely a mentor, taught me a lot about what I know and what I do here at Pi with philanthropy and community engagement.

Doing both jobs allowed me to expand and to operate nimbly, because I didn't need to pay myself a salary, which was a huge benefit to the operation in the first few months. I never took any income from the restaurant the whole time I was at Salesforce. I only had to pay my partner.

I thankfully can claim to have quite a bit of balance these days because I have surrounded myself with a great team. They operate the restaurants day in and day out, so I'm back to being the corporate guy. Well it's not necessarily corporate, but it's more office time. I spend my time behind a desk instead of on the floor, which in some ways is disturbing, but it's the only way to operate four stores.

What are you focused on?

You can either choose to operate or you can choose to expand, and I've chosen the latter. I'm still the face of the business, and I am still in the place. But I am generally in there more socially than I am to supervise. Thankfully my guests and my regulars understand that I'm not going to be there, and they don't seek me out any more. It's no longer a disappointment to some of the original regulars that Chris isn't there, and they understand.

We still have some great loyal people from day one, many of whom got really upset when we started getting more and more successful after the first presidential experience that they couldn't get into the restaurant. But now that we have a few more locations, they can still get a table.

How did President Obama find out about Pi?

That goes back to '07 when I flew home to St. Louis from San Francisco for a fundraiser for the then-Senator at a friend's house. Many of my friends and family laughed, thinking it was foolish because nobody knew who this Barack Obama guy was.

So I met long-shot junior Senator Barack Obama and his assistant, Reggie Love. I kept in touch with them, and when Reggie would come out to San Francisco, we'd go out and get drinks or dinner.

Fast forward to October of '08 when I found out the Senator was coming to town for a big rally. Reggie and I were talking and I said, "Hey, I've got the pizzeria opened. Would you guys be interested in some pizza?" He said, "Hell yeah!" and told me he'd have the advance team contact me. They didn't contact me until the morning of, and they put in an order and said they would send somebody to come get it.

I think the pizza sat for a couple of hours in the heat behind stage, but afterwards as I was walking down the street to catch the train home, Senator Obama called and said it was the best pizza he had ever eaten, or something to that effect. We joked about the irony of eating deep dish pizza in St. Louis, and what that might do to Chicagoans, and in fact it did have a little bit of a negative effect for him. So that was October of '08, and he was elected President in November.

In March of '09, Reggie called and said the President wouldn't stop talking about our pizza, and he asked if we would come in and bake it in the White House. So we got some über security clearance and we were actually able to bring in some of our own ingredients. At first they were going to buy everything for us because everything the President eats, they have to procure. But they got us a level of clearance that we were actually able to bring our dough on a plane, and then the rest of the ingredients we bought at Whole Foods when we got to D.C.

We spent seven hours in the kitchen. We baked about 20-25 pizzas, and fed the President, his family and a lot of his staff. Then we got to hang out with him for a little bit in the Roosevelt Room. We've since fed him three or four more times. When he comes to town they generally just order and don't tell me until after the fact so they don't have to get secret service clearance, since I don't know about it.

He and his whole staff have been extremely gracious, and it's done wonders for my business. Obviously it's a huge honor, and thankfully he does have good taste in pizza!

That's a huge honor. Congratulations!

Thank you. We have been very fortunate. There are a lot of people who work very hard in this business and who are very talented that don't get a break like that.

We were doing very well and looking to expand to our second store before this happened, but nobody can deny how that launched us onto the national stage and gave us a lot of national press. Whether people agree with his politics or not, they are obsessed with what the first family does. Since the Obamas are considered to have good taste and take their food very seriously, it's that much better for us. So we have been extremely fortunate, and we recognize that it is a unique situation.

You've been smart to strike while the iron is hot. Let's switch gears and talk about partnerships. How do you make partnerships work?

I've been fortunate in that aspect as well. I recognize that it's easier to get along when things are going well. But at the same time, Frank, is considerably older than I am, and I worked for him when I was in high school and college. I knew his work ethic. I knew his level of service. I knew his design and business background. But there were still a few unknowns.

I think a lot of times people like to enter into business with people they like to drink and hang out with. Maybe their kids get along. Maybe they happen to be family. But I had worked with him before, and I had known him almost 20 years. I just knew if I was going to do this there was only one person who could run this for me while I was still at Salesforce. I was still very active, but I would not have been able to do it without him.

So I didn't have to learn along the way about who he is professionally, and I think that's what a lot of people find out in relationships that go south. They realize that they knew their partner socially or in a familial way, but not professionally.

Not to say we haven't had bad moments. We upset each other I'm sure almost daily. But at the same time, we know we are in this together and we couldn't do it without each other. Each of us brings something else to the table.

I have been very fortunate that he doesn't mind not being the face of the business. He is mature enough that he doesn't let his ego get in the way and get bitter that I am the front man of the company, so I am grateful for that as well. His ego and my ego have never clashed in that way.

So both of you anticipated having those roles, and you being the face of the business?

I don't know that we anticipated it, or if Frank was just cool with it because he was mature and was being taken care of and finding satisfaction with it. You know, I was the money behind it, but at the same time he had more to give up than I did because he was older and had a career and a family, so it was a bigger risk for him than it was for me to piss away some money on a restaurant that wasn't going to be successful.

But again, I knew him and he was beyond that age where being front and center would have mattered to him.

You started Pi without any debt?

Correct. I was fortunate enough to make money in Silicon Valley, and was able to pay cash to open it. But we are opening in D.C. this spring, and that will be the first one where we have an architect and we have a general contractor and we have sub-contractors. Otherwise, Frank and I have been the designers and the general contractors and the project managers for every one of our stores. We've been able to do it inexpensively, and people think our build-outs cost much more than they did.

But that's why we've been able to do it, because we've been able to cut costs on lots of things. Now we're giving up a little bit more of that. We'll still design to a significant degree, but we will have a proper architect for all of our future stores, so we will have to hand over that piece that we have enjoyed. It's stressful for everybody, but it's the natural evolution. It's like any business. As you grow, you have to figure out what you hand over and what you delegate. Being able to delegate has also been a huge part of our success.

Delegation is tough for a lot of people.

But necessary for growth. At Salesforce I was pretty much an individual contributor, so I was sort of the low man on the pole. To have more than 300 people work for me now is very different.

It's two different paths and personas. When I was at Salesforce, I learned that in order to be successful, I have to hand over pieces. Certainly there are going to be stumbles along the way, but you can't train people to replace yourself unless they have opportunities to take on things and grow with you.

We've been fortunate that we have been able to hand over a big piece of our operations to various individuals so that we can focus on growth and getting the other stores open. We have people that we can hand things off to, because they have been given responsibilities along the way.

How much planning went into Pi before you got started?

Pretty significant planning. We weren't sure if we were going to take investors or not. When we were out seeking money, it wasn't a good time to do that, so I'm glad that we did not take on money. But since we were considering it, we did put together a plan, and we labored over it quite a bit, from the language we used to the design of the presentation, to the numbers and the pro-forma. We leveraged tools from Restaurantowner.com, and other things that we were able to gather from people.

We put quite a bit of time into it, and we still go back to it from time to time. It's kind of fun to see that it did happen, and it isn't too far from what we envisioned and what we got down on paper.

How do you manage growth effectively?

I'd love to be able to predict the future four or five years out. We are going to open a company-owned store in Washington, D.C. in 2011. We also have some licensees who are looking to open elsewhere around the country.

We struggle with growth. There are lots of offers of money and lots of interest. But there is money, and there is smart money. We haven't exactly figured out what the proper mix is. We know that we want to strike while the iron is hot, but we also don't want to dilute and expand too fast. We've been pretty fortunate so far, and we don't want to jinx that.

We know we could continue to open one to two stores per year ourselves, and we may continue to do that. We know that there is a lot of interest outside of our ownership in doing this elsewhere, so we put together a team. We have a hospitality director and other individuals who can support the out-of-town network.

By growing so fast, we didn't have all of our standard operating procedures down, so I have hired some good multi-unit people who have helped us backfill and put together a package. We use it ourselves for future growth, and we can hand it off to a licensee. I feel like we are now poised to be successful out of town.

I give a lot of weight to reviews and anecdotal feedback from people out of town who think that the product would work elsewhere. I don't want it just to be a St. Louis phenomenon, so I want feedback from guests who are from out of town. That's almost more important to me now. It makes me feel like we're not just a one-trick pony, or a one-town phenomenon.

We're just trying to be smart and prudent, and make sure there are not too many cooks in the kitchen, and that we don't get heavily leveraged. It's nice to use other people's money for growth, but at the same time it gives us a lot of flexibility when we don't have to answer to anybody or service a lot of debt.

I saw a YouTube video you made about sustainable business practices. What things are you doing to keep your business green?

I think the latest one you might have seen was our adoption of the Green Box, which is a licensed technology from Eco Incorporated out of New York. It's made of 100% recycled material and it's a 100% recyclable pizza box. It's hard to find both of those together.

But an even cooler feature is that the top of the box is perforated and breaks into plates, and the remainder of the box folds into a wedge to keep the remaining pizza in your fridge and take up less room. It eliminates the need for extra packing materials, like foil, to keep your leftovers. It's simple, but at the same time it's kind of ingenious. It's great for us because we have a lot of carry-out business at a couple of our stores and from our pizza truck. It's great. It's sort of all-in-one.

We've been buying carbon offsets from day one. All of our stores are mainly filled with reclaimed and upcycled materials. Whether it's the material in the flooring to the art, with environmentally friendly paint, to super low-energy light bulbs, to everything we could do with recycled material.

We also recycle about five-to-one to our landfill waste, and have begun composting recently. So about 80% of what comes out of our kitchens is recyclable. We pay pretty heftily to have that recycled here in St. Louis because they don't provide that service.

We also only have draft beer. One of the biggest contributors to the landfill is the glass from beer at places like our pizzeria. By not having bottles, we eliminate the waste in the first place, and we don't have to recycle it. We're the largest beer account for many distributors here. It just makes sense. I think draft beer is the right solution anyway. Draft beer is inherently sustainable because of the re-use of the keg.

So being "green" is a very important part of your concept?

Yes. It's part of our core DNA. I would encourage anybody that's thinking about getting into the business to think green from day one. We even have a green mission statement that sits on our menu right below our regular mission statement.

You need to get people thinking along those lines from day one, because it's harder to teach an old dog new tricks. So if you make it a critical decision factor from day one and get your staff on board, you're going to be much more effective at it.

Two and a half years ago when we were starting off, we were pretty forward thinking. Thankfully, two and a half years later it's not that forward thinking. We're still probably ahead of the curve over 90% of the restaurants out there, but nowadays you don't find too many restaurants opening that aren't doing something environmentally friendly. It is just critical to make sure that it is factored into every decision you make, from vendors to products to design and build out.

It will cost you a little bit of money up front, but ultimately will save you a lot of money, and I think it is the only way to own and operate a business.

You have a philosophy of accountability and transparency. Why is that important?

Our hospitality mission is about communication and transparency. We don't get upset if people make mistakes, as long as we know about them before I hear about it the next day from a guest, or on the website, or through social media.

I think you have to have that in any organization, especially in an organization with more than 300 employees, and four and a half locations (including the truck). We use Schedulefly for a lot of that. On the scheduling. On the shift trades. On overtime and keeping labor costs in order.

We have a philosophy that you don't win alone and you don't lose alone. So keeping everybody informed, keeping the manager informed, and letting everybody know what's going on helps us operate and keep the ship afloat when it could become unwieldy. As long as you inform your manager if there is a potential for a table to be unhappy, we can fix the situation and nip it in the bud.

What are some of your other core philosophies?

We live and die almost from the book called *Setting the Table*, by Danny Meyer of Union Square Hospitality Group. Our managers all get a copy of it, and we constantly refer back to the legendary hospitality that he writes about, and writing the last chapter. We can't write the last chapter unless we know about it – unless there is transparency and honesty in our business.

So that's part of our DNA, and that philosophy is not limited to the restaurant business. You've got to be honest, you've got to be transparent, and you've got to be accountable.

What's another technology you use other than Schedulefly?

I wake up in the morning knowing exactly what happened at all of my stores because it's automatically emailed to me using a web-based technology called Formstack. I know what happened on the guest front, I know about any employee incidents.

I don't get an email or a phone call from an employee who was terminated three days ago. I know about it upfront, in real time, because we are being accountable and we're being transparent. I may not be present in the restaurant, but my staff is keeping me fully informed.

Technology has really helped us. Even for side work. It sounds so silly, but at the end of the night they check a box on an online form and certify that all side work has been completed, and so I know that that restaurant is clean. They are signing their name on a form, and that makes them accountable.

It's amazing how much better my operation is because we hold people accountable. It works. Everybody knows what's coming, and they know the expectations we have for them and what they can expect from us and how we handle situations.

What are you doing along the lines of philanthropy and community engagement?

We set a goal to give about 1% of our revenue back to the community, in the form of in-kind donations and cash donations. We do organized food drives and team volunteer events.

To an extent, we pick organizations that are near and dear to me to support. But at the same time, we know that it's all about our guests, and what's important to them. A lot of it is stuff like gift certificate donations to auctions, and food donations, and a good amount of cash as well. And again, that has been a part of our core DNA from well before we were profitable. It also pays for itself in other ways of course.

We created a reputation for being involved in the community from day one. There are certainly causes that we prefer to give to, but if it's important to our guests, then it is important to us because we look at them as partners in the whole thing, and we owe our success to them.

We are also in the process of putting together our own 501(c)(3) charitable organization right now for things that need to be done at the corporate level. So we'll have our own non-profit.

We're also starting to show up with our truck to do benefits and events for non-profits. And finally, to drive people to our online ordering, we're donating 50 cents of every order to a "non-profit of the month." We also let people add a donation to their online order like you would see in a grocery store and other similar efforts.

Again, like the green thing, it's got to be a part of your core DNA and your operating model.

Before we started the interview, you mentioned the phrase "Evolve or die." It seems like a lot of restaurateurs fail to change with the times.

Yes, the world is flat in every industry. If you look at fashion and what people are wearing, or what people are eating, the lag between when it shows up on a runway or in a progressive city and when it appears in the heartland is shorter than ever.

Stagnating is only going to get you so far. It used to get you maybe 20 or 30 years with one business, but it's not going to any more. People are more informed and their palates are more sophisticated. Their dollars are more stretched. You can't get comfortable.

When I talk to some of my other restaurateur buddies – especially the successful ones – they tell me you have to have a healthy level of paranoia that you are not keeping up. It can be to your demise if you go overboard with it, but you have to keep thinking about innovation. Recognize what's really important to you and don't change things that continue to be winners, but at the same time, recognize and offer new things.

For instance, we have vegan options, and we have gluten-free beer and a gluten-free dessert. That kind of thing is becoming more and more important. If you are inclusive, then those people with allergies, or people with religious limitations, or whatever else, are going to be your biggest champions.

Many of the new things come from listening to our customers directly, or anecdotally, or just keeping an ear open to what's going on in the marketplace.

As I said, I built my restaurant around a deep dish recipe, and most everything else on the menu is ours. But we are not afraid to borrow and to emulate what's going on elsewhere, and I think you are a fool if you don't.

Do you look outside of the restaurant industry for ideas?

Oh yeah. Technology is near and dear to my heart, so I pay attention to what I do in the cloud with Schedulefly and other technologies, or what I do with social media.

As I said about the book *Setting the Table*, those philosophies apply to anything. We're all sales people to some degree. We're all providing hospitality in one way or another. So, yes, I do pick up on things in every business I go to.

We talk about this stuff all of the time. We also talk about what's going on in other segments of our industry too. We talk about what it's like going to McDonald's. We talk about fine dining. We talk about what's going on at the pizzeria around the corner. Again, you're kind of a fool if you don't.

Unfortunately a lot of restaurateurs can't afford a team in place that enables them to go out and visit other people's establishments like I can, but that is really critical. If you don't incorporate what you see elsewhere – whether it's what you eat, or what you experience yourself – if you don't dine out a lot, it's hard to keep up.

Whether it reinforces something that you are doing well, or drills home the fact that you are failing somewhere, it's just a constant discussion. I'm getting ready to have my core manager's meeting with my senior management team, and a lot of what we discuss in those meetings is what we experience elsewhere, and not just what happens in our stores.

You have more than 300 staff. How do you find people that share the same passion for your business that you do?

It starts off on our job application asking "Why is Pi important to you?" I don't want to hire somebody who has not at least done their research and can't come up with something creative.

We've made mistakes in the past though. We've hired too quickly because of our growth. But we are not afraid to turn people away. I can't control every service interaction, but if I don't see that they share our passion, or that they are smiling, or that they enjoy their job, then unfortunately they are gone. I have a lot of loyalty to people that share our vision, but we have to make a lot of painful decisions as well, and we have to trim the fat very frequently.

We now have a multi-staff hiring process. We have somebody from senior management interviewing everybody, down to server assistants. It's not that we don't trust our GMs to make the right decisions, but we are trying to help them make better decisions.

From the moment people walk in, we'll tell them, "Sell me Pi." We are all selling something, whether it's the person trying to up-sell an order or just dropping off a water glass. We are all selling Pi. We are all selling the experience.

We want people to ask themselves, "What would Chris do?" And it's not just about me, it's about what would any owner think. We ask people to think like an owner, and think outside the box. We want them to do things like walk the plant in the morning and find the cigarette butt that you didn't think was there.

We also talk a lot about first impressions. First impressions of people. First impressions of the plant. When I am dining somewhere and I see something that looks untidy or unclean, I think about what the kitchen looks like. I'm not a details guy when it comes to my life, but I am very detailed when it comes to the aesthetics of my restaurants and the people in my restaurants.

Highlights - A quick recap of Chris's key points...

- ✓ Delegate your way to success

- ✓ Make being "green" a core part of your DNA

- ✓ Internal communication and transparency are critical

- ✓ Evolve or die

- ✓ Dine in lots of other places

- ✓ Make job applicants do their homework

Preparation, hiring integrity over experience & putting on a nightly production

Jim Parker
(with co-owner Mary Beth Dooley)

Red Hat on the River
65+ employees
Irvington, NY
Restaurant owner since 2003
www.redhatbistro.com

Jim co-owns Red Hat on the River with his wife, Mary Beth Dooley. He left a very successful, 25-year career in the movie and film production business in 2003 on a whim to start a small bistro in Irvington. Seven years later, Jim and Mary Beth are at their restaurant seven days per week, and they make the hard work and passion they pour into it look easy to the many guests they serve every day. Red Hat has established itself as an institution, so much so that people have been known to take the 30-minute train ride from Manhattan to dine there. The Clintons have even visited – twice. Jim told me that when he started, he knew nothing about restaurants, and he learned as he went. It's pretty clear he has learned quite a bit...

How did you get started in the restaurant business?

We moved from Manhattan up here to Westchester County about 20 years ago to raise our child. My wife and I had both worked in film production. I was a line producer and she was an executive producer. I spent my career in film production eating in restaurants, so I had a pretty good idea of what I liked, and it inspired me.

I fell in love with Irvington. It's a very quaint, hilly village of about 6,000 people right on the Hudson. It's absolutely beautiful and picturesque. It was always a very peaceful place in contrast to my very busy film production life.

In 2002, a little pub on Main Street in Irvington had fallen on hard times. I thought it could be a fun little quaint bistro. I called up a buddy of mine who was in between careers and asked him if he would be interested in joining me in this venture. He said, "Yes." So we put a little money together and started renovating.

My wife and I had been very involved during our production careers in building sets and transforming locations for film shoots. We had an understanding of the importance of imagery. We were always looking for a place to eat, and we wanted to go to a place that was somewhat sophisticated. So to me, it was all about creating the place where we, as diners, would want to spend our time. We had a lot of fun with that. My wife is an amazing designer. She designed this restaurant and the original one on Main Street. We had nobody else doing it except us, and it's really her eye that captured the feeling that we wanted to project to our audience.

So, we started renovating in late 2002. The building was built in the 1850s. There were holes in the floor and tree trunks holding up the building. And, as is typical, when you start to re-do one thing, you find something else that's wrong, etc. I hadn't signed up for this, but at the end of the day, I completely rebuilt two floors of somebody else's building. Of course it would have been great if I owned the real estate.

At that point we were pretty deep in debt, and my partner decided he didn't like the idea anymore and he bailed. So we had to make a decision. Do we go full-tilt boogie and become restaurateurs, which I knew nothing about? Or do I go back into the film business? Well, we opened in June 2003.

I've always liked change, and I've always embraced new projects. I don't ever want to regret passing on an opportunity to do something new. And I really did believe in it and knew there was a market for a neighborhood bistro. So at the end of the day, I stayed with it, and my wife and I just did it together. It was a slow build, but after 3½ years we had gained a modicum of success.

Why did you leave your career in film for the restaurant business?

I had a really successful career in the film business, so here was no reason for me to do something different. It's just that I'm always looking for a new project, and I always had a passion for the restaurant business.

It was only because I was driving and saw an open storefront that I had the idea. If I'd seen an open storefront in the town three miles away, I wouldn't have done it. It was only because I love my town so much. It was close to home and I loved the building. In fact, it had been an eatery for close to 100 years. During prohibition, it was an ice cream parlor, and they used to do shots in the back. It had a really checkered history. [Laughs]

So it was for all of those reasons that I left my film career. In fact, I said to myself, "Maybe I shouldn't do this. I've got a kid in college." And then I thought, "Ah, screw it. Let's see what happens." [Laughs]

How did you learn how to run a restaurant?

I did not know what I was doing. I learned by fire. I think that my background in film production was a perfect primer for coming into this business. It was a perfect thing to do, short of being in culinary school or restaurant/hotel management. The restaurant business is very theatrical. I feel like every night, the curtain goes up here. We try to create an engaging atmosphere for every single person who comes in. This is their leisure time, and they've chosen to spend it here, and I take that really, really seriously.

What's your philosophy on what makes a restaurant successful?

I have a little bit of a different bent on things because I didn't grow up in the restaurant business. I had been a customer all of my life. So I'm flattered by the fact that people take the time to come down to where we are and choose to spend their money with us rather than somewhere else.

And how many times can people go out a week? I don't know. Maybe it's once every two weeks. But whatever it is, it's very flattering that people choose to come here. And we're very careful to make sure our staff understands that. A lot of young folks that work in the restaurant business don't realize that when two people want to go out for dinner, and maybe leave their kids at home for the evening, it can be quite costly. Babysitters. Gasoline. Dinner. So every step of the way, we want that experience to be perfect.

Obviously, without good food, you're done. But we worry about our customers' good time as well. It's all about the sound, the imagery, the hospitality and the charm of our whole staff. So if I had to put it in a couple of words, I would say that besides the obvious – the food – it's all about the casting and the script.

Our casting is our staff, and they're fantastic. They're fantastic because they take their jobs seriously and they want other people working with them to take their jobs seriously. In a way, it's kind of self-policing. We've been very successful in that respect.

Now that I finally learned the restaurant business after seven or eight years, I'm feeling very comfortable with it.

When you started in your first location, how did you finance it?

I got a small, under $100,000 loan. It was a small, 50-seat place. We kept repairing, fixing, renovating, and upgrading, so the loan disappeared pretty quickly. Over the four years we were there, we chipped away at the debt and paid it all off, but we must have borrowed an additional $250,000 or so. Home equity and credit cards played a roll.

You moved to your current location a few years later? How did you finance that opening?

When we came down here, I went and found lenders. People who saw us grow as a business on Main Street and who had come to know us. That, and a third of our own money, got us going. We kind of go through a high and low season and it was a big investment upfront. So, getting through the low season can be pretty hard, especially if you're not properly financed. I find every which way to get my vendors to extend credit to me through the winter time, I have a good relationship with a small, regional bank, and all of that kind of stuff.

Having built relationships over the first few years, everybody knew me. And it's all just worked out well. It's almost like a fairy tale. Now we're doing huge numbers. Much more than I had ever thought.

All of those years of using credit cards, borrowing from friends and getting credit lines. But I knew this would work. I would have never stayed on Main Street. That was over. Because now that I understood the type of restaurant we were running had high food costs, etc., I couldn't make a living in a 50-seat restaurant. But it set the foundation for the place we're in today. It's almost like that was my college, and now I'm in the master's program.

Business is hopping now?

Yes. This is a pretty serious place that has a lot going on. We get some pretty interesting people that come here. The Clintons have been here twice. All of the county executives. Lots of celebrities, movie actors, sports figures. The novelist, James Patterson put us in three of his Alex Cross books. So there's a lot of notoriety for our place now.

If you have a good product, you just keep growing. It's like a domino effect. So three years in, I'm very pleased with our movement.

It's funny because people that don't know the background will come in and think it looks pretty easy. I don't ever want the public to see me sweat, but I'll tell you something, I sweated for several years.

What did you learn about partnerships when your partnership failed?

You know how you can't afford an apartment when you're younger, so you take on a roommate? Then you realize that you've got to live alone, and you even pay more rent just to be able to do that. You want to have one opinion, as opposed to sharing it.

I had known my partner for 20 years. But all of a sudden, I knew him in a different way. So I would never go into something like that again, unless it was someone I had worked with in this business. For instance, I have a manager that has been with us for seven years. I wouldn't want to function without him. I could. But I wouldn't want to.

He's been through all of those periods with me here in the restaurant. And now, we're talking about what we want to do in the next five years. And I would go into business with him in a heartbeat. I know him. I know his family. I know his parents. I know the girl he's about to marry.

That's the difference. When you get to know all of those folks that surround the people that you want to go into business with, I think it's a very helpful indication of who they really are. It's also very helpful that we've worked together for seven years now, in the heat of battle.

My original partner was somebody I knew as a family friend. But I did not know him in the heat of battle at all.

How do you find the right people to work for you?

By not just finding people to fill a role just because they can perform some of the duties. When people walk in here looking to work with us, I worry more about their personality, and their integrity, and their charm. And I don't really care if they can do the job or not. At least not initially.

I have to make sure that whoever every single customer deals with — whether it be a busboy, a floor runner, the food runner, a host, etc. — has to be engaging, and has to care about that person being in our space.

Life is too short. The person's dining experience is too important. I can't afford to have people who have another agenda. I want everybody to have another life, so they become an interesting person to be around. And I ask everybody to read The New York Times every day if they can, because we leave it on the bar. And I want everybody to engage in stuff like that, because I want them to know what my sophisticated customers know.

We have a lot of interesting, curious people that work here. If I had to put it in to a couple of words, I like having curious people around me.

What have you learned that has surprised you?

I come from a very organizational background in terms of film production. In that business, if you don't do everything in preparation, you're done. I find that most people I work with don't have that experience.

I anticipate and live the experience before it happens. It's a little bit like I can't sleep at night, which is a little bit annoying because you never rest. So I envy all of those that don't think that way and can sleep, but I do think it's the key to being successful in some respects.

Sharing that perspective with the people I've worked with for a long time becomes helpful, because preparation becomes a way of operating. It's like saying, "O.K., we see how many reservations are coming in. We know we have these groups coming in. We also know a bunch of the different folks, and they're kind of anxious about where they sit, or what they drink, or what they eat." That's one of those nights where everything is going on at the same time. We sit with everybody and talk about that so that everybody can get in it their head what's going on. Then we figure out how we can move people around, so we can figure out how these people can be happy here and those people can be happy there.

In a lot of ways, what we do is very personal. I don't treat the restaurant as, "We have X amount of seats, and we have X amount of people coming in, and one way or the other, we're going to figure out where to put them."

It's all about being hospitable and making it work for people by making them feel comfortable and letting them know we're going to solve any problems. I find it to be real simple. It works a lot better when I get a lot of sleep. [Laughs] But at the end of the day, the most important thing we can do is be flexible and understand the needs of all of our guests all of the time. Otherwise, what are we doing this for?

Most restaurants fail. Conventional wisdom would have indicated that you probably would have failed because you had zero experience and went into debt. How did you succeed when so many fail?

I think at times it's because those who run small businesses can't see beyond their original concept and are reluctant to take off the blinders, and I don't think they understand the public as much as they should. Maybe they need to get out more, which, by the way, is not so easy in this business!

I don't want to sound like I'm putting other restaurateurs down because I'm not. There are plenty of people in the restaurant industry whom I absolutely look up to. And I'm enamored with their modus operandi, and all that they've achieved.

On the other hand, when you go into a restaurant to enjoy a meal and you're ignored, it's so obvious to me why the dining room is not full. As a customer, when you are ignored, you start to wonder what else they are ignoring. If you're going to ignore the guests, you're probably going to ignore all of these other things.

It doesn't matter if you have a trendy looking place, or a cool looking bar, or the greatest chef in the world. You have to engage the people that come into your place, day after night after day after night, and remember who they are, and why you're here.

My wife and I work almost seven days a week. Since we do it together, and we're always here together, it's fine. She is very bright, and she recently said, "This is a lifestyle. This is more than just owning your own business." And since it's a lifestyle, you have to know that everyone you come in contact with at any time of day either wants to know you, or wants to be a part of your place. It's like being on a stage.

Between the two of us, my wife and I make every effort to engage all who come through the door. And we are members of the community, so we started that way in our little, humble place up the street. Folks would walk in, and we would engage them. We would talk to everybody. We would tell them what we were doing, and why we were doing it. And we really cared about it.

I'd like to say that I was really smart, and had a plan, but I didn't have any plan. The only thing that worked for me was that I felt like I knew what people wanted. So I got lucky.

It sounds like you and Mary Beth set good examples for your staff to follow.

I think people have a tendency to emulate people that are in charge, or that are successful, or that they respect. I certainly did as I grew up.

Did your lack of experience help you in some ways?

Yes. I remember when I first started – and even sometimes now – I had people telling me, "But you can't do it that way, because that's not the way it's done." I didn't care what anybody said. I mean, I listened to people I respected, and I took their advice where appropriate, but I followed my instincts.

What kind of marketing do you do?

I'm a big believer in marketing. People say, "I see you everywhere." Well, they don't. But that's the perception. It's similar to how you see the GE logo or the AT&T logo. You see it everywhere. You don't even know what it means, but you get the impression that it's a good company because that logo is everywhere. My wife and I come from a background where we did a lot of commercials, so we have a sense of that, and we apply that.

Of course, we're a sophisticated restaurant so we didn't go down the road of coupons or all-you-can-eat buffets. That's not who we are. We created this restaurant so people living in suburbia can come in and feel like they're in Manhattan and not have to go into Manhattan.

We make a lot of charitable contributions. When we first started it seemed like everyone came to me looking for a charitable donation for their fundraiser. And I'm thinking, "I can't afford this. Who do I give to, and who do I not give to?" And then I realized how worthwhile it would be to just give every request within a 50 mile radius $50. Good marketing and good community relations. People would say, "Well, we want dinner for four." Or, "We need an ad for $250." I'd say, "We don't do that." So instead of discriminating, I just decided to give the same amount to everybody. We give a lot away every year. But it's real simple to figure out, and I just look at it as part of the advertising budget.

I also advertize in publications in certain areas that I think are appropriate. I'm relentless about ad placement. I drive editors nuts. I want someone to open a newspaper and for their eyes to go right to page three (right side) where we have our ad. That's what I'm concerned with. Advertising is important year-round but most critical in the slow times.

Haven't you also built good relationships with several large companies near you?

Yes, we cater to a lot of large companies that have offices in the area. Siemens. Kraft. IBM. They come for corporate dinners all of the time. Even for a party of 10, we will create a unique menu for their event and even print a custom menu with their corporate logo and the evening's selections. We get to know these companies. They've become a very important element to the business. We try very hard to accommodate all of their needs. For example, on the day they're coming in, we'll find out if they are coming from a meeting, or having a meeting. A lot of the time, they may have just gotten off of an airplane from a 16-hour flight from Asia. We will try not to seat people around them so they can have a little peace and quiet.

What do you have in mind for the future?

We're talking about a place that's done more simply, maybe more artisanal with fewer employees. Right now, we have 85 employees in the summer and around 55 during a typical northeastern winter. So it might be nice to have another place that compliments this place, but has 10 employees.

Highlights – A Quick Recap of Jim's Key Points...

✓ Put on a nightly production

✓ You'll sweat – just don't let 'em see it

✓ Know how your potential partner works in the heat of battle

✓ Hire integrity and charm over experience

✓ Delivering excellent customer experiences is an art, not a science

✓ Staff will do as you do

Community, filling voids
& being transparent with your staff

Arch Rock Fish

60+ employees
Santa Barbara, CA
Restaurant owner since 2010
www.archrockfish.com

You've probably seen Scott Leibfried on TV. A well-renowned chef, Scott is currently on the hit FOX Network television show "Hell's Kitchen" on the FOX Network. He evaluates and consults with Gordon Ramsay on all of the restaurants on FOX's "Kitchen Nightmares," and he has appeared several times on The Food Network's series "Party Starters." He co-owns Arch Rock Fish with Jeremiah Higgins – who I also interviewed for this book – as well as MLS and Team U.S.A. soccer star Cobi Jones. Scott, Jeremiah and Cobi also run HJL Group

Restaurant Advisors. Scott has been working in the restaurant business since he was a teenager. He has a hunger for knowledge, tons of passion, an incredible work ethic and valuable wisdom and insight into what it takes to be successful in his business. A few of his thoughts are below...

How did you get involved in the restaurant business?

I come from a small town in New York, on Long Island. It just always seemed to me the obvious opportunities were to move to Manhattan and become something. I could always be a police officer, or a fireman, or a construction worker or something like that, but I felt that eventually my calling would find me.

I started working in hotels and restaurants as a teenager just as a part-time summer job, and it helped me find a path that I was very, very interested in. Starting as a bellhop or a busboy, to my first job in an actual kitchen – making salads, cutting vegetables, and that kind of stuff. It always felt very comfortable. It always felt like a place where I should be.

Ironically enough back then, when I first started in this business 18 years ago it was never looked at as an industry with any sort of future. You started working in a restaurant or a hotel, and you did that until you retired. You usually retired with not much of anything, if you were lucky to retire at all. It was never looked at as a career path that would take you anywhere at all, except to just give you a job.

You didn't buy into that?

No. I never believed that because I always thought it was fascinating. I was always exposed to a different part of the business that the average person didn't really know much about. What I saw were opportunities to meet people, to travel and try different things, and to explore other countries and other cultures, all from a food point of view. To me, that was very fascinating, and where I wanted to focus most of my energy.

So that's what I did. After graduating high school and working in a couple of restaurants, I tried a community college program for a little while, and it didn't work out. One day while I was at my restaurant job, one of the chefs pulled me aside. He said, "You really enjoy doing this, I can tell." I said, "Very much so. I think this is what I want to do." He said, "I graduated from Johnson & Wales culinary school in Providence, RI a couple of years ago, and you might want to check it out. It might be a good place for you to go. I had a really good experience, and learned a lot, and it's a very reputable learning facility." He wrote me a really nice recommendation, and I ended up getting in.

Was that a worthwhile experience?

Absolutely! I took a two-year course. At that time, that was the program. Now it's actually turned into a four-year bachelor's degree.

Where did you go next?

When I graduated I stayed in Providence for a while, and lived outside of Boston while I was trying to figure it out. At the same time, a friend of a friend suggested I check out this place called Martha's Vineyard, which was a stone's throw away.

My understanding was that it was a great place to spend the summer and work, and people made good money. You worked hard for the summer, but you ended up walking away with a pocket full of money. Anybody at 22 or 23 years old would be interested in that.

I ended up getting my first sous chef job, and it was a wonderful experience. I met a lot of great people, and that's where I really started to get my eyes open to the travel part. I started meeting people from Australia, New Zealand, Ireland and from all over the Northeast. I found myself surrounded by an eclectic group of people, but all restaurant people.

That's when I got a taste of what the business is all about from a personality point of view. These people were from everywhere. We'd work hard all night then go to the beach and hang around a bonfire and drink beer, laugh and have fun. We'd get up early in the morning, maybe try to catch a bass or jump in the ocean, and then do it all over again. Some of the best memories of my life.

But still I was able to do everything I wanted to do. I was able to be employed by some independent owners that really struggled at times to keep their businesses afloat, and that was the part of the industry I wanted to learn.

I also wanted to learn the unappreciated craft of cooking – about food and culture and the experience. That's when I decided that I couldn't be that corporate person that you're supposed to be when you graduate college.

You spent five years there. Why did you leave?

At that point, I needed to fulfill a void in my life professionally, and I thought it was time for me to move to a big city. I was reading a lot in the newspapers about The Patina Group, Wolfgang Puck and the European movement in New York City.

Looking back on it now, it was the beginning of what we now know as the restaurant business. Fresh food, creativity and innovation were center stage. My wife, who was my girlfriend at the time, and I looked at each other and said, "Where do you want to go?" It really came down to heads, New York, and tails, California. So we flipped a coin. It ended up being tails, and we decided at that moment we were moving to the West Coast.

We settled in Los Angeles. It took a little bit of time to figure it out, and I started the interview process. I knew my tremendous amount of experience and my East Coast work ethic would take me far. Through the process, I was offered a high level cooks position from The Four Seasons Company, in its flagship property in Beverly Hills.

I really thought about that opportunity, and said to myself: "It's a great company. Very stable. Very professional. A lot of European chefs, and people from all over the world. This is a great opportunity, and the learning experience will be amazing." The company was very reputable. One of the best at that time.

I accepted a high-level cook position, and within six months I was promoted to a sous chef position. Within a year, I was responsible for the banquet department. I was doing well over $12,000,000 a year in annual revenue. I had everything I wanted. The knowledge. The experience. The people.

I was fortunate to be involved in two new hotel openings with the company, and see the process from start to finish. It was an amazing process.

Sounds like you got tons of value from that experience.

Absolutely. It was a great company to work for. Tremendous opportunity, great people. But at a certain point, I had to decide what I was going to do next. I really wanted to move around, and there wasn't much mobility at the company at that time, and that kind of forced me to look outside.

I got a lot of interest from boutique restaurant companies, and I felt very comfortable with Tavistock Restaurants and jumped in. They had about 28 locations at that time. I had a great tenure with them as well, and ran one of their busiest locations – a $5,000,000 location in Westwood.

But again, the opportunity to look around again came because there wasn't really anywhere else for me to go at that point. I started getting a lot of independent work from people who were asking me to help with openings, and organization, and recipe creation, and a lot of different things. So I just independently survived for quite a few years, surprisingly, without having too much stress, and really trying to figure out what it was that I wanted to do.

Through working independently as a consultant, I was hired by Santa Monica Seafood, to brand a new café in a retail store in Santa Monica. Michael Cigliano was a long-time friend, as well as colleague, and he gave me a call one day. I had lunch with him, and at the end of lunch, he said, "We're doing this big deal down in Santa Monica. We're renovating and building a brand new retail store. It's state of the art. It's in a beautiful location. We're really excited about it, and we're also going to build an oyster bar and a café inside the retail store."

In most of my younger years in Cape Cod and Martha's Vineyard, and growing up in Long Island, we had clam chowder all of the time. We had lobster rolls. We had fried clams. Nobody on the West Coast ever really knew what these things were, and it shocked me. So I decided to help Michael, and my idea was to expose the West Coast to simple East Cost seafood. We branded the café, and it came out better than I had ever expected. It grossed double what we had projected the first year. It's very busy, and people absolutely love it.

I knew that was going to be a good stepping stone, because I had always wanted to open my own little oyster bar, and just have it be very simple. Just raw oysters, and iced shellfish, clam chowder, and lobster rolls, and just really be able to manage it, and put a handle on something that I knew was very simple, and that I knew I could do and that I wanted to do.

I don't want to wear a starched white chef's coat. I don't want to wear a big tall hat. I want to wear a t-shirt, put on my apron and have a good time with the people I'm working with, and enable us all to learn, make money, and have fun. That's really the only thing that I ever wanted to do on a regular basis.

That's where you met Jeremiah Higgins?

Yes, and we hit it off right away. There was an understanding, an energy and a chemistry. It was a very positive working experience, and I really enjoyed it. We had a great time.

Jeremiah and I started spending a lot of time together and talking about our ideas and goals. We both started getting excited about our conversations and the possible future we could have doing what we really wanted to do. We would talk about current trends and where we see the industry going related to food and operations. We wanted to prepare for the next big swing in the industry that will involve technology. Technology that we wanted to simplify for the restaurant owner, chef and staff. Blogs, video, testimonials and web cams were just the beginning of what we were thinking. We have many goals set forth for ourselves, including the growth of our restaurant concepts.

We were approached by a gentleman that we worked with to reorganize a few of his restaurants and bars. He was working on negotiating a lease on a space that he felt had potential to be something special. It was an existing restaurant that spent a small fortune on the renovation and then went out of business shortly after. We never want to hear about owners that have had to close their doors, but the second owner usually receives all the benefits from the first owner. He wanted to talk to us about it. We walked the space, and we started throwing some ideas around. At the end of that day, Arch Rock Fish was born.

Partnerships often fail. How do you make a partnership work?

Honesty and hard work. I am a workaholic, and it is difficult to find that quality in co-workers and partners. I'll go days and days without doing anything except working. I don't think everybody has that quality. When you find people that have that quality, it ends up being a respectful relationship. At that point, you have to look around and say, "These are the people that I think I would be able to work extremely hard with, and get along with, because they understand that part of it."

And it's not a one-sided relationship, where one person is responsible for everything. It's two people working for one common goal.

Why is the failure rate so high with restaurants?

I think a lot of it has to do with poor planning, and a bit of the unknown. Once you start construction, you do not know what you will find behind walls. Equipment can be delayed by weeks or months. Permits take time to get issued and inspections can lead to

297

more unknowing. I think people view opening a business as easy and glamorous. It's very hard work, and your commitment needs to be 100% of every minute of every day.

A lot of times they're underfunded going into it, and then half way through they don't have any money to complete any of their construction, or to train any of their staff prior to opening. There are a lot of little things that come into play. But I think if we were to sum it up in one thought, planning and contingency is very important.

Do you have to stay ahead of the curve and constantly be willing to innovate to succeed long term?

Partially. I think it depends what your concept is. Conceptually, some people create something that's going to stand the test of time, and they do it intelligently. I think if you want to be cutting edge, hip and cool, you're walking a very thin line, because that calls for reinvention every few years.

I look at guys like The Palm Steakhouse, and Morton's, and McCormick & Schmick's. Some of the chains have done very well based on having an idea that they've stuck with, and by creating something that fills a void in the marketplace. We want our concepts to be comfortable, fun and set ourselves apart with great food with a value attached to it.

Once you get out of that, and you try to perceive yourself as being chef-driven, or food-driven, and not considering the entire business as a whole – whether it be the ambiance, or the beverage program, or the concept itself, or the culture of the company behind it – then you run into problems. When you don't consider those things, and develop those things accordingly to implement what the guest is going to see, then, yes, you will find yourself trying to reinvent yourself way more often than you should.

If you come up with something that everybody can understand, then you're less likely to need to reinvent yourself. Maybe not the next biggest thing, but just something that's very good. Something that's very casual. And something that people can feel comfortable with, at a price point that is perceived as a value. That was something that Jeremiah and I had always agreed upon.

Look at places like Frank & Musso's in L.A. That's the oldest restaurant in Hollywood. They're still doing the same thing they were doing when they opened up their doors 45, 50 years ago, and people still love it for what it is because they can rely on it. They can count on it.

How do you find employees that share your passion for your restaurant?

You have to search and search and search, and you have to talk to a lot of people before you find the one or two that were meant to be.

Again, there's this misperception of our business. There's a lot of entitlement. A lot of people don't understand the hard work that goes into it. If you are patient, you'll eventually find yourself surrounded by the people that truly are passionate about it. You just have to be patient. You just have to keep looking ahead. Eventually, you will find each other.

It's usually through mutual contacts. A lot of times it's through the vendors that I have a longstanding relationship with. They're the ones that can really give me a yes or a no on somebody, because they've seen them, or have known them in the past.

I understand that transparency with your staff is important to you.

Yes, I'm very open with the members of the staff on this project. I tell them how much the debt is. I tell them exactly what we need to do in order to pay the debt off: Be very successful, make more money individually and be a popular restaurant that everybody in town loves. I don't try to keep anything from them because I want them to understand exactly what they're up against, and I want them to work hard for their own success as well. I think that's part of the internal motivation for them. I think they really appreciate that honesty and that openness, and that they're going to continue to learn.

You have focused a lot on being a part of your community

Absolutely. And we repeatedly told people and reminded ourselves that we're not just a couple of guys trying to open a restaurant. We want to be a part of this community. We want people to have their graduations here. We want people to have their anniversaries with us. We want people to walk off the beach after just meeting a couple of people, and come in for a couple of beers at happy hour. We just want everybody to feel comfortable here, without feeling like it's a club, too stuffy or not casual enough.

Your community focus led you to pair up with the Police Activities league as well, right?

Yes, we thought it would be a nice idea to pair up with a charity in town. What other way to seem like you're part of a community, than to be a part of a local charity? The Police Activities League was the first one that came to my mind. My father served as a police officer, and I was very familiar with the organization.

The members of the league got very excited, and we said, "Let's do some promotional stuff. Let's do some things to bring in some money to you guys." We're on the forefront of their minds, and they're on the forefront of our minds. It was really one of the smarter things that we did. They're all great people, and it just all worked out.

What's your long-term goal?

We want to develop two other concepts that are very similar to Arch Rock Fish and concentrate on growth. Appropriate growth. We also have an additional idea that we are very passionate about that will take a little time to complete, but we will get it done.

The goal is to have a medium-sized restaurant company that we are proud of.

Highlights – A quick recap of Scott's key points...

✓ Honesty and hard work are a must

✓ Effective planning and contingency will mitigate failure risks

✓ Try to fill a void in the marketplace

✓ Look hard for the right teammates - don't settle

✓ Be transparent with staff

✓ Partner with a charity to help you get engaged in your community

Hiring effectively, opening your curtain
& focusing on volume over profit margin

Arch Rock Fish

60+ employees
Santa Barbara, CA
Restaurant owner since 2010
www.archrockfish.com

Arch Rock Fish is not your father's fish house. Serving simply grilled fish, artisan and locally sourced food, local California wines, and offering warm service – it's a true neighborhood joint. Jeremiah is focused on turning it into an institution in Santa Barbara. He rose quickly through the ranks, starting as a teenage busboy, and becoming a general manager by the time he was 20. Since then he has led success after success, helping turn around and grow several well-known restaurants in Los Angeles and Santa Barbara. He co-owns Arch Rock Fish, and also helps run HJL Group Restaurant Advisors with Scott Leibfried and Cobi Jones. Jeremiah is a high-

energy, optimistic, upbeat guy who works extremely hard, is a fantastic leader, has a great business mind and exudes success. It's a pleasure to close the book with this awesome interview...

What's your background in the restaurant business?

I never really planned on going into the restaurant business. I think it's a business that chooses you, and you're either good at it or you're not. It will chew you up and spit you back out if you're not right for it.

Like a lot of people, my very early years were spent bussing tables. I worked for a famous jazz musician, Terry Briggs, who opened a little restaurant on the beach in Santa Barbara called Sea Cove Café. He had the restaurant for about 10 years, and he would bring in live jazz musicians every night, seven days a week.

I was a busboy. It was a lot of fun. Always busy. That was when I was 17. After about a year, he made me a manager, and then the general manager within about two years. So that was my first real restaurant job.

I had always had a love for the arts and film, and one day Terry said, "You should go to film school. You should follow that passion." So I quit that job when I was 21 or 22, and went back to bussing tables at the Enterprise Fish Company, also in Santa Barbara, and went to Santa Barbara City College.

I had never been a good student before, but I was focused on getting into film school, so I studied very hard, made the Dean's List, and graduated with a 3.9 GPA. In high school I think I had a 1.6 or so. I was just terrible.

Enterprise Fish had a sister restaurant in Santa Monica, so I moved down to L.A., worked for them serving tables, and got into USC (University of Southern California) Film School. At the same time I worked for Miracle Pictures and Alex Kitman Ho, a famous Oscar-winning producer who produced movies such as *"Platoon"*, *"JFK"*, *"Born on the Fourth of July"* – basically all of Oliver Stone's movies before 2000.

I was managing at Enterprise Fish Company, and going to school and working for Miracle Pictures. When I finished school in 2000, all of Hollywood went on strike. Meanwhile, I had about $110,000 in school loans, so I started working full time at Enterprise Fish Company as a general manager, to pay my bills off while I was waiting to go back to work in film.

The owners then offered me the general manager position back in Santa Barbara, so I told them I'd take it for six months, to wait out the strike. Plus I figured I could pay off about half my bills.

That led to a turn of events for you, right?

Yes. About three months into the job, I sat down with the owners. At that point, they had been open about 25 years and sales were flat. Both owners were honest with me, and told me that times were tough, and they may close a store.

Because they had been honest with me, and I felt their pain at the prospect of these successful stores possibly failing after such a long run. I was determined for that not to happen, and I said, "That's not gonna happen. I'm going to do $3,000,000 in sales for you this year."

They laughed at me. I can understand why. I was promising to raise sales 40% over the prior year. They basically patted me on the head and said, "O.K. kid. Sure that's gonna happen." But it did. We actually went over that goal by $8,000 on the December 31 of that year.

A 40% jump in sales is enormous for one year. How did you do that?

I motivated our staff. I looked at our sales daily, at what days were slow, at what hours were slow. I looked at goals for the month, for the week, for the day.

I basically started breaking things down, and looked for the spots that needed to be filled in. I realized that areas where we were slow in sales were opportunities, rather than areas for discouragement. Most managers think every Monday has to be slow because it's a Monday. I would look at Monday and say, "Let's make Monday just as popular as Friday, for a different reason."

So that's basically what we did. I involved the staff. I also involved the locals. We really went after them, rather than the tourists. We made it a place that everyone enjoyed coming to regularly.

So you must have had growth opportunities after that?

Yes, I was then offered the general manager position at the Santa Monica store, in addition to continuing as GM in Santa Barbara, so I took that challenge as well. I was splitting my time between both of the two stores, and then the owners took me to another restaurant they owned called Hurry Curry of Tokyo, and I thought the concept was amazing. They gave me that one too. [Laughs] So now I had three under my control within one year.

You were able to manage all three successfully?

Absolutely. Without disclosing financial information, in five years we took the company up 120% in sales, just by approaching it with enthusiasm, engaging the staff, and engaging the customers and guests, and making it their place to go. And by just running a good business. A tight business.

We not only grew sales, but we made the company strong and profitable as well. We went from being in the red by a couple of points, to averaging 17% profit per store.

And I don't take the credit. I give the credit to the management and the staff that I was lucky to have worked with over the years there. I think every single person over those years played a part in what we did.

Were you still pursuing film production on the side?

At that point I didn't really look back at film. I guess I just realized that this was a really good business to be in, and if you could be good in this business, you could run any type of business.

It has a lot of similarities to the film business. You're going on stage every day. Each day is a brand new day, and a brand new show. The money is tight. The margins are really tight. The staff is your cast, and your job is to inspire them every single day to get the results that you want. You've got to look at people individually, and figure out what motivates them, and then just pay attention to the details, and run a tight, clean business. If you do, you'll be successful.

There are a thousand moving parts in a day, that's what excites me about the business.

How did you wind up at Santa Monica Seafood with Scott Leibfried?

I got a call from Michael Cigliano, who co-owns Santa Monica Seafood with his brothers and sister. I think they are the second largest seafood purveyor in the country. They may even be number one by now.

I had bought seafood from Michael at Enterprise Fish Company, and he watched as Enterprise transformed, and sales started going up. He called me up in 2007, and asked me to come open up his new flagship store on Wilshire Boulevard – a 10,000-square-foot seafood store, market, wine store, and café. I agreed to give him six months and open the new store while we continued to look for locations for our project. It's probably the biggest project that I have worked on to date. It's the most beautiful design. I've never seen a market quite like it.

I was there for one year, and that's where Scott and I met. He and I struck it off. He has the same drive, and the same desire to serve great food in a casual environment. He was working on *"Kitchen Nightmares"* and *"Hell's Kitchen,"* and my friend Cobi Jones – who I had been talking to about starting a restaurant – and I went to visit him on the set. We sat down and just decided to form our consulting group, with the intention of opening a concept that Scott was working on, called "West Coast Oysters."

We formed HJL Advisors – Higgins, Jones, Leibfried. The day I walked out of Santa Monica Seafood, after having been there one year, I got a call from a gentleman named Mark Lawrence in Santa Barbara. He had been buying up a lot of restaurants, and taking advantage of the down market and locations.

So I drove to Santa Barbara, and started the project the next day. I spent four months on the project, and put operations tools in place, and trained the staff with their manager's help.

Our consulting group started getting quite a bit of work with Mark. We helped open four restaurants in six months, and I thought we were done doing work for him, but he showed us another building that he wanted to purchase. It had been a Melting Pot, open for one year. It was basically brand new.

We had been looking at locations in Los Angeles for the West Coast Oysters concept, but Mark positioned this location to us as a perfect place to work out the kinks in our concept. So we put together a pre-opening budget of what we needed to make it look like what we wanted it to look like, and to market it the way we wanted to market it. Mark gave us total freedom to create a cool concept. You couldn't find a better partner than that.

So here we are. We're opening up tomorrow night.

How did the slow economy impact your planning?

We consciously thought about the economy. Seafood places typically have higher food costs, and higher plate costs. They are more of a special destination in an economy like this. But we learned at Santa Monica Seafood to price everything at $15 and under. We almost tripled our sales projections by doing that there because people saw that as a value, and we still made a great, great profit because we were doing volume. I've always said to anyone that we advise in the restaurant business "You don't put percentages in the bank. You put dollars in the bank."

Yeah, it's great to have a 32% food cost. But if you don't have any money coming in, then what's the point? So we've always operated under the philosophy that volume is very important. If you do enough volume, then the bottom line is always healthier than it would be if you lived and died by those textbook food cost analyses, and things like that.

So you've carried that philosophy to Arch Rock Fish?

Absolutely. We decided going into Arch Rock Fish that we were going to give up a few points on our food costs, and reduce our menu costs by a couple of bucks.

What other philosophies are you taking into Arch Rock?

One of the other philosophies going into this has been to make it accessible to anybody. Not only in comfort and design, but it's also a true neighborhood place. We're going to know your name. I'm going to know everybody that walks through the door, and so will our staff.

And we don't want to throw down a check that's so big that we only see you on special occasions. I hope to see you two or three times a week. Maybe it's lunch one day, happy hour another day, and dinner once a week. I think we've built a menu and place that nobody is going to have a hard time coming to, and they won't have left half their wallet here when they walk out the door.

What have you done to create awareness?

That's one of the things that I am proudest of.

There are so many great ways now to market a restaurant with little money. My plan was always to use everything from cell phones to Twitter to Facebook to word of mouth, to get that buzz going at a grass roots level.

We get a lot of press because of it. Over a dozen articles around town (In Santa Barbara) have been written about us before we've opened. Most of the writers say, "You've got 1,000 friends on Facebook, and you're not even open." To me, that's not a lot, but it's still a great sign that we are reaching people, and that we do have brand awareness. I spent $12,000 on pre-marketing. The rest of it's all been free press and word of mouth.

How about an example of what you've done?

For example, one of the questions I get a lot is, "What does it take to open a restaurant?" So we thought we'd use Facebook and blogs to document what happens, from the start to the end.

We showed a history of what it takes to open a restaurant. Our guests can see where Arch Rock Fish came from, from choosing our silverware and our plateware, to our menu, to the purveyors.

I think that this is a relatively new way of looking at a business. A business owner usually does not want to share what happens behind the curtain, or let anyone see the little man cranking the wheel. It's usually a very protective kind of a thing. We decided that we were going to do the opposite. We decided we wanted to show everybody, from day one, behind our curtain.

We also mentioned our purveyors in the press. We didn't do one interview where we didn't mention Jordano's, or Telegraph Brewery, or Brian from the Santa Barbara Fish Market, or some of these big purveyors that we use. We brought them down to share our success, and to get some press themselves.

To us, the term "A Neighborhood Joint" isn't just a phrase. It means helping our own local community thrive, by promoting the people around us. Not only our restaurant, but the restaurant across the street.

That's certainly unconventional.

Why not? You promote me, I promote you. Why not build that kind of relationship with your vendors and other people out there? I don't understand why you wouldn't do that. There really is enough to go around. And more will go around, the more excited people get about where they live and what they're doing.

You aligned Arch Rock Fish with the Police Activities League. Why just one charity?

I was giving $200 here, and $500 there, and I never really know if it makes a difference. So we decided to choose something that made sense to the Arch Rock Fish concept, and made sense to the partners. Helping kids stay active in sports was what we thought made sense.

Around here, the main activity the PAL sponsors is soccer. PAL takes care of kids that can't afford uniforms, or can't afford fees to join the different athletic events. We announced right off the bat that they were our charity of choice. And with Cobi Jones being a famous soccer player, it just fit.

All of this stuff led to us having a big base in Santa Barbara before we open our doors. We've got great brand recognition. It's very encouraging to see how much you can do with very little, just by going back to some of the basics.

What new technologies excite you?

Foursquare [a mobile phone-based, interactive city guide and discovery application] is a good example. That program has made it easy to get excited about checking in at a restaurant, and sharing your experience.

It's the same thing with Schedulefly. I see two or three posts a day where the staff is talking to each other, or we're posting notes to them, or we're communicating better with them.

In a way this has to do with technology, but it's kind of back to basics. People are actually talking to each other. For a while it was nothing but email, and that was so impersonal. But now there are some fun applications that get you involved in your community again, and get you involved with your friends and your peers, and help you see what everybody is doing.

Many restaurant partnerships fail. How do you avoid that?

First of all, you've got to get along with your partner. You're going to basically live with a business partner at a restaurant. You're going to spend 10 to 12 hour days, minimum, with this person. So before I thought about partnerships, I thought about people that I share the same philosophy with. People you can laugh with. People you don't get too stressed being around. People who have a mutual respect for others. Not only in the way that they speak to staff and the people around them, but that they enjoy life and respect others. So that's the basics.

At the end of the day, to have a successful partnership, you've got to have common goals, and you've really got to know that person inside and out before you go into partnership with them. You've got to know how they react to different stress levels, and different problems that arise, because there will be problems in a restaurant. You're gonna put out 10 fires a day. It's how you and your partners deal with putting out those fires, and how you deal with problem solving, that will help make a strong partnership.

How do you find people to hire that will convey the same passion and love you have for your business to your guests?

I'm glad you asked that question, because hiring the right people is one of the most important things that restaurant operators do. Here's what I do personally...

I think the interview process has to be a structured, minimum three-part process. Over the years I've noticed that when I like somebody right off the bat and I give him or her the job, they usually end up being the first to go. They either don't want the job, or they don't show up for their shifts, or they take advantage of it when they do. They're not the person I thought they were when I hired them. Over the years I've learned that people will do better if they earn the position.

I like for them to speak to an assistant manager, then to a manager, and finally, to an owner. So far, I've always asked that I have the last decision on who gets hired. You're never too busy to take 10 minutes to spend with that employee before you hire them. Most owners don't do that. They leave it up to management to decide. But management may not have the same outlook as an owner does.

So, number one is I would put them through an interview process that's structured. Number two is I would meet everybody before they are hired. And the third thing is the easiest. I don't care what's on a resume. I go off of personality.

If that person engages me in the first two minutes, with a twinkle in his or her eye, or a smile, or a good story, or whatever it happens to be, they're going to engage my customers. If they don't have that personality, if they don't have that enthusiasm and that twinkle in their eye, I can't teach them that. It doesn't matter what concept I have, I can teach them the procedures, the menus, the wine lists. I can teach them how to serve a table correctly, and how to say goodbye, and all of that. But I can't teach personality. So the number one thing that I look for is personality.

Hiring the right people is so important. The nationwide average is about $2,200 to hire and train somebody. Why make a mistake? Why spend all of that money, and then have to do it all over again a week or two later? And that $2,200 doesn't even account for the cost of lost customers if that server is not the right person at your table, and it's turning off customers.

Highlights – A quick recap of Jeremiah's key points...

✓ Turn slow days or slow times of day into opportunities

✓ Running restaurants is like making movies

✓ Focus on volume over margins

✓ Promote your community, not just yourself

✓ Show people what's behind the curtain

✓ Hire personality over experience

Thank you to the stars of the book...

Thank you to the 20 incredible stars of *Restaurant Owners Uncorked*. You spent time not only participating in the interviews, but also in reviewing your transcripts, answering my follow-up questions, steering me to your contacts to help me promote the book, and so on. You are all very busy running awesome, successful, profitable, fun restaurants, and I greatly appreciate the time you gifted me. Anybody who reads this book will benefit enormously, learn a lot and be better at what they do because of each of you. You are all badasses, and you all inspire me.

Thank you to you, the reader...

Thanks so much for reading our book. We hope you learned something, or got inspired. Or both! If you'd like to hear more from some of these owners and others, please check out our incredible **Restaurant Owners Uncorked Video Series** on our blog:

http://blog.schedulefly.com

Schedulefly

[sched·ule·fly]

- *noun*

1. A company with a passion to make life easier for independent restaurant owners, managers and staff.

2. A simple web-based software that makes it easy for restaurants to schedule staff, communicate and get organized.

Reviews

"Schedulefly is fun." – Murray Brothers Caddyshack

"Staff LOVES it." – Mikuni Japanese Restaurant & Sushi Bar

"Schedulefly rocks." – Mickey Mantle's Steakhouse

"Schedulefly pays for itself two or three times per month." – Partners II Pizza

"So easy to use I've never needed any help." – Pacific Coast Burritos

We created Schedulefly specifically for restaurants, and we have a laser focus on helping them.

We mostly serve independent restaurants. More importantly, we serve people who like to keep things easy and fun! We have a simple web-based service with a familiar interface – not too many screens, buttons or settings. We have only added the stuff that really matters – thoughtful features that restaurants can actually use.

We're currently three guys in three different cities in North Carolina (Wilmington, Raleigh and Charlotte). Since we keep things intuitive, we don't need many people to help take care of our customers. This makes our business nimble, and a blast to run.

We don't have investors, so nobody is breathing down our necks to grow faster. Instead we grow one restaurant at a time, and we take great care of our customers. In fact, 99% of them renew every month.

If you own a restaurant, we would love for you to join the rapidly growing family of Schedulefly users! Check us out at **www.schedulefly.com**.

Wil, Wes & Tyler
The Schedulefly Crew

Design

Luke Pearson is a master at visual storytelling, and he designed the cover of this book. He also doctored up the pictures of the owners to include their names, and he is the guy who created the customer video on the home page of our web site at www.schedulefly.com. He's done other incredible work, which you can find at www.liftfilms.net. Luke lives in Cary, N.C., and you can reach him at lukepearson@liftfilms.net, or 919-738-5455.

Editing

Colles Stowell is a veteran writer, editor and website consultant, and he cranked out the editing. He added a lot more value than I thought any editor could. He's easy to work with, works fast and provides great advice. On several occasions I declined his edits, because I tend to be stubborn. So if anything in this book doesn't read well, that's on me. Colles lives in Wilmington, N.C., and you can reach him at cstowell@tightlineswriting.com, or 603-674-9620.

Made in the USA
Lexington, KY
06 February 2013